DANGEROUS planet

DANGEROUS planet

The Science of Natural Disasters

2

El Niño to Landslide

· · · · · · · · · · · · · · · ·

Phillis Engelbert

AN IMPRINT OF THE GALE GROUP

DETROIT · NEW YORK · SAN FRANCISCO
LONDON · BOSTON · WOODBRIDGE, CT

Dangerous Planet: The Science of Natural Disasters
Phillis Engelbert

Staff

Diane Sawinski, *U·X·L Senior Editor*
Carol DeKane Nagel, *U·X·L Managing Editor*
Thomas L. Romig, *U·X·L Publisher*

Kim Davis, *Permissions Specialist*
Robyn Young, *Project Manager, Imaging and Multimedia Content*
Pamela A. Reed, *Imaging Coordinator*
Robert Duncan, *Senior Imaging Specialist*

Cindy Baldwin and Pamela A.E. Galbreath, *Senior Art Directors*

Rita Wimberley, *Senior Buyer*
Evi Seoud, *Assistant Manager, Composition Purchasing and Electronic Prepress*

Marco Di Vita, Graphix Group, *Typesetting*

Cover photographs: (front) parched land reproduced by permission of The Stock Market, volcano reproduced by permission of JLM Visuals, and tornado reproduced by permission of FMA, Inc.; (back) hurricane and wildfire reproduced by permission of Corbis Corporation.

Library of Congress Cataloging-in-Publication Data

Engelbert, Phillis.
    Dangerous planet : the science of natural disasters / Phillis Engelbert ;
        Diane Sawinski, editor.
    p. cm.
    Includes bibliographical references and index.
    Contents: v. 1. Avalanche to earthquake - v. 2. El Nino to landslide - v. 3.
        Meteorite to wildfire.
    ISBN 0-7876-2848-4 (set) — ISBN 0-7876-2849-2 (v. 1) — ISBN 0-7876-
        2850-6 (v. 2) — ISBN 0-7876-2851-4 (v. 3)
    1. Natural disasters — Juvenile literature. [1. Natural disasters.]
I. Sawinski, Diane. II. Title.

    GB5019 .E54 2001
    363.34–dc21   98-54422

Printed in the United States of America
10 9 8 7 6 5 4 3 2 1

table of contents

Table of Contents

reader's guide

Since the beginning of civilization, humans have tried to make sense of the natural phenomena that have claimed so many lives and continuously changed the landscape of planet Earth. From avalanches to wildfires, *Dangerous Planet: The Science of Natural Disasters* explores the real-life stories and scientific explanations behind these processes that have proven to be destructive to humans, wildlife, and their surroundings.

The natural disasters in *Dangerous Planet* are discussed from scientific, sociological, and historical points of view. Up-to-date information on technological advances in predicting and forestalling natural catastrophes is provided, and the most recent gains in understanding the causes of these disasters are explained.

Scope and Format

In three volumes, *Dangerous Planet* is organized alphabetically into the following sixteen chapters:

Avalanche	Blizzard
Earthquake	Drought
Dust Storm	Flood
El Niño	Global Warming
Hurricane	Landslide
Meteorite	Monsoon
Tornado	Tsunami
Volcano	Wildfire

Each chapter is divided into sections covering significant disasters in history; explanations of the scientific processes causing the disasters; the consequences of that type of natural disaster; the role of human activity in the disaster; technology used to predict, prevent, and respond to the disaster; and tips for survival in the event the disaster strikes.

Dangerous Planet: The Science of Natural Disasters features boxes containing fascinating disaster stories and eyewitness testimony. Charts and tables present statistical data, and approximately two hundred photographs and illustrations keep the volumes lively and entertaining. Additionally, *Dangerous Planet* contains a glossary, sources for further research, and a general index that gives easy access to all the subjects, events, and people discussed throughout *Dangerous Planet: The Science of Natural Disasters*.

Acknowledgments

Thanks are due for the invaluable comments and suggestions provided by the *Dangerous Planet* advisors:

Kevin Finson, Professor, Science Education,
Western Illinois University, Macomb, Illinois

Joseph Hoffman, Science Teacher,
West Bloomfield High School, West Bloomfield, Michigan

Chris Gleason, Science Teacher,
Greenhills School (grades 6–12), Ann Arbor, Michigan

Stephanie Karr, Math and Science Teacher,
Orchard Lake Middle School, West Bloomfield, Michigan

Donna Miller, Media/Instructional Technology Coordinator,
Mesa County Valley Schools, Grand Junction, Colorado

Special thanks also go to Renee McPhail, wonderful friend and research director; U•X•L Senior Editor Diane Sawinski; copyeditor Chris Cavette; advisors Chris Gleason and Stephanie Karr; writer Rob Nagel, who prepared original drafts of the Earthquake and Avalanche chapters; and the individuals who sustain the author daily—William Shea (husband), Ryan Shea (son), and Bob (cat).

Comments and Suggestions

We welcome your comments on *Dangerous Planet: The Science of Natural Disasters*. Please write: Editors, *Dangerous Planet: The Science of Natural Disasters,* U•X•L, 27500 Drake Rd., Farmington Hills, MI 48331-3535; call toll-free 1–800–877–4253; fax to 248–699–8097; or send e-mail via http://www.galegroup.com.

words to know

A

Acid rain: rain that is made more acidic by sulfuric and/or nitric acid in the air due to the burning of fossil fuels.

Active volcano: a volcano that continues to erupt regularly.

Aftershock: ground shaking that occurs after the main shock of an earthquake.

Air mass: a large quantity of air throughout which temperature and moisture content is fairly constant.

Air pressure: pressure exerted by the weight of air over a given area of Earth's surface. Also called atmospheric pressure or barometric pressure.

Alps: mountain system composed of more than fifteen principle mountain ranges that extends in an arc for almost 660 miles (1,060 kilometers) across south-central Europe.

Andes: mountain range extending more than 5,000 miles (8,045 kilometers) along the western coast of South America.

Anemometer: instrument used to measure wind speed.

Aquifer: an underground layer of spongy rock, gravel, or sand in which water collects.

Arid: a climate in which almost no rain or snow falls.

Ash: very small, fine fragments of lava or rock that are blasted into the air during volcanic explosions.

Asteroid: a rocky chunk of matter in orbit around the sun.

Asthenosphere: region of Earth's atmosphere below the lithosphere, composed of partially melted rock.

Avalanche path: the course an avalanche takes down a slope, composed of a starting zone, a track, and a runout zone.

Avalanche wind: a cloudlike mixture of snow particles and air pushed ahead of a slab avalanche as it races downward.

B

Backfire: a small fire set by firefighters in the path of an oncoming wildfire to burn up the fuel before the main fire arrives, thus blocking it.

Barometer: instrument used to measure air pressure.

Basalt: a type of rock that forms from hardened lava.

Blizzard: the most severe type of winter storm, characterized by winds of 35 miles (56 kilometers) per hour or greater, large quantities of falling or blowing snow, and low temperatures.

Blocking system: a whirling air mass containing either a high-pressure system (a blocking high) or a low-pressure system (a blocking low) that gets cut off from the main flow of upper-air westerlies.

C

Caldera: a large depression, usually circular or oval shaped, left behind when a volcano's summit collapses.

Cinder: a small piece of material thrown from a volcano during an eruption.

Cinder cone: a volcano made of lava fragments.

Clear-cutting: the logging practice of harvesting all trees from vast forest tracts.

Climate: the weather experienced by a given location, averaged over several decades.

Cloudburst: the heaviest type of rain, in which rain falls at a rate of 4 inches (10 centimeters) or more per hour.

Coalescence: the process by which an ice crystal grows larger. The ice crystal collides with and sticks to water droplets as the ice crystal travels through a cloud.

Coastal flood: a flood that occurs along the coast of a lake or ocean.

Cold front: the line behind which a cold air mass is advancing, and in front of which a warm air mass is retreating.

Comet: a body in space that has a tail made of rock and ice and follows an orbit around the sun.

Composite volcano: a volcano with steep sides made of layers of lava and ash.

Cone: the sloping walls of a volcano (not all volcanoes have cones).

Conelet: a small cone on the side of a large volcano.

Conservation tillage: the practice of leaving vegetation in farmed fields during idle periods to protect the soil from erosion and trap moisture.

Continental drift: the geologic theory that all continents were originally part of a single landmass before they slowly separated and drifted apart.

Convection: the upward motion of a mass of air that has been heated. Convection is the primary way that heat is transferred in the atmosphere. It is the process by which warm air rises up from the ground, to be replaced by cold air. The cold air is then warmed and cycles upward.

Convection current: circular movement of a gas or liquid between hot and cold areas.

Conventional radar: instrument that detects the location, movement, and intensity of precipitation, and gives indications about the type of precipitation. It operates by emitting microwaves, which are reflected by precipitation. Also called radar.

Crater: the bowl-shaped area around the opening at the top of a volcano.

Crest: the highest point of a wave.

Crown fire: a fire that spreads through the treetops, or crown, of a forest.

Crust: the outermost layer of Earth, varying in thickness from 3.5 to 50 miles (5 to 80 kilometers).

Cumulonimbus: (pronounced cyoom-you-lo-NIM-bus) a tall, dark, ominous-looking cloud that produces thunderstorms. Also called thunderstorm cloud.

Cyclone: (pronounced SIGH-clone) the name for a hurricane that forms over the Indian Ocean.

D

Dam: a barrier built across a river or stream that blocks and controls the flow of water.

Debris avalanche: a downward slide of loose, earthen material (soil, mud, and small rocks) that begins suddenly and travels at great speeds—similar to a snow avalanche. It builds into a fearsome mass of mud, trees, and rocks that can cause much damage.

Deforestation: the removal of all or most of the trees from a region.

Dendrite: a starry-shaped snowflake that has accumulated moisture and developed feathery branches on its arms. A dendrite is the most distinctive and most common type of snowflake.

Deposition: the process by which water changes directly from a gas to a solid, without first going through the liquid phase.

Desert climate: the world's driest climate type, with less than 10 inches (25.4 centimeters) of rainfall annually.

Desert pavement: hard, flat, dry ground and gravel that remains after all sand and dust has been eroded from a surface in the desert.

Desertification: the process by which semiarid lands turn to desert. It is caused by prolonged drought, during which time the top layers of soil dry out and blow away. Also called land degradation.

Doppler radar: a sophisticated type of radar that relies on the Doppler effect, the change in frequency of waves emitted from a moving source, to determine wind speed and direction, as well as the direction in which precipitation is moving.

Dormant volcano: a volcano that has not erupted for many years.

Downdraft: downward blast of air from a thunderstorm cloud, felt at the surface as a cool gust.

Dropwindsonde: a device that is released at a high altitude by an aircraft in order to transmit atmospheric measurements to a radio receiver as it falls. Also called dropsonde.

Drought: (pronounced DROWT) an extended period during which the amount of rain or snow that falls on an area is much lower than usual.

Dust Bowl: the popular name for the approximately 150,000 square-mile (400,000-square-kilometer) area in the southern portion of the Great Plains region of the United States. It is characterized by low annual rainfall, a shallow layer of topsoil, and high winds.

Dust devil: a spinning vortex of sand and dust that is usually harmless but may grow quite large. Also called whirlwind.

Dust storm: a large cloud of dust blown by a strong wind.

E

Earthflow: a landslide that consists of material that is moist and full of clay, yet drier than the material in mudflows.

Earthquake: a sudden shifting of masses of rock beneath Earth's surface that releases enormous amounts of energy and sends out shock waves that cause the ground to shake.

Ecosystem: a community of plants and animals, including humans, and their physical surroundings.

Effusive eruption: the type of volcanic eruption in which lava spills over the side of a crater.

Ejecta: the stream of rock and dust that is thrown upwards when a meteorite strikes a planet.

El Niño: (pronounced el NEE-nyo) Spanish for "the Christ child," this is an extraordinarily strong episode (occurring every two to seven years) of the annual warming of the Pacific Ocean waters off the coast of Peru and Ecuador.

Electric vehicles: vehicles that run on electric batteries and motors instead of gasoline-powered engines.

ENSO: acronym for El Niño/Southern Oscillation, it describes the simultaneous warming of the waters in the eastern Pacific and the shifting pattern of air pressure between the eastern and western edges of the Pacific Ocean.

Epicenter: the point on Earth's surface directly above the focus of an earthquake, where seismic waves first appear.

Erosion: the removal of soil by water or wind. This is especially harmful when the top layer of soil, called the topsoil, is stripped away, because this is the layer where plants grow.

Eruption: the release of pressure that sends lava, rocks, ash, and gases out of a volcano.

Extinct volcano: a volcano that is expected never to erupt again.

Eye: the calm circle of low pressure that exists at the center of a hurricane.

Eye wall: the region of a hurricane immediately surrounding the eye, and the strongest part of the storm. The eye wall is a loop of thunderstorm clouds that produce heavy rains and forceful winds.

F

Fair-weather waterspout: relatively harmless waterspout that forms over water and arises either in conjunction with, or independently of, a severe thunderstorm. Also called nontornadic waterspout.

Fall: the downward motion of rock or soil through the air or along the surface of a steep slope.

Fault: crack in Earth's surface where two plates or sections of the crust push and slide in opposite directions against one another.

Fault creep: slow, continuous movement of plates along a fault, allowing pressure to be released.

Fire line: a strip of ground, cleared of all combustible material, that is dug by firefighters to stop the advance of a wildfire. Also called control line.

Fire triangle: the combination of three elements required for any fire: fuel, oxygen, and heat.

Firejumper: a specialized firefighter who parachutes from airplanes to strategic locations to battle wildfires.

Firestorm: the most explosive and violent type of wildfire. Also called blowup.

Fissure: a crack in Earth's surface through which volcanic materials can escape.

Flash flood: a sudden, intense, localized flooding caused by persistent, heavy rainfall or the failure of a levee or dam.

Flood: the overflow of water onto normally dry land.

Floodplain: nearly flat land adjacent to a river that is naturally subject to periodic flooding.

Focus: the underground starting place of an earthquake. Also called the hypocenter.

Foehn: (pronounced FANE) a warm, dry wind that flows down from the Alps onto the plains of Austria and Germany.

Food chain: transfer of food energy from one organism to another. It begins with a plant species, which is eaten by an animal species; it continues with a second animal species, which eats the first, and so on.

Foreshock: ground shaking that occurs before the main shock of an earthquake.

Fossil fuels: coal, oil, and natural gas—materials composed of the remains of plants or animals that lived on Earth millions of years ago and are today burned for fuel.

Frostbite: the freezing of the skin.

Fujita Intensity Scale: scale that measures tornado intensity, based on wind speed and the damage created.

Fumarole: a vent in Earth's surface that releases steam and other gases, but generally no lava.

Funnel cloud: cone-shaped spinning column of air that hangs well below the base of a thunderstorm cloud

G

Geologist: a scientist who studies the origin, history, and structure of Earth.

Geyser: a regular spray of hot water and steam from underground into the air.

Glacier: slowly flowing masses of ice created by years of snowfall and cold temperatures.

Global warming: the theory that the average temperatures around the world have begun to rise, and will continue to rise, because of an increase of certain gases (called greenhouse gases) in Earth's atmosphere.

Global water budget: the balance of the volume of water coming and going between the oceans, atmosphere, and continental landmasses.

Great Depression: the worst economic collapse in the history of the modern world. It began with the stock market crash of 1929 and lasted through the late 1930s.

Greenhouse effect: the warming of Earth due to the presence of certain gases in the atmosphere, which let sunlight come in but don't let heat go back out into space—as if Earth was covered with a big glass greenhouse that keeps everything warm.

Greenhouse gases: gases that trap heat in the atmosphere. The most abundant greenhouse gases are water vapor and carbon dioxide. Others include methane, nitrous oxide, and chlorofluorocarbons.

Ground blizzard: the drifting and blowing of snow that occurs after a snowfall has ended.

Ground fire: a fire that burns beneath a layer of dead plant material on the forest floor.

H

Haboob: (pronounced huh-BOOB) a tumbling black wall of sand that has been stirred up by cold downdrafts along the leading edge of a thunderstorm or cold front. It occurs in north-central Africa and the southwestern United States.

Harmattan: (pronounced har-ma-TAHN) a mild, dry, and dusty wind that originates in the Sahara Desert.

Heat cramps: muscle cramps or spasms, usually afflicting the abdomen or legs, caused by exercising in hot weather.

Heat exhaustion: a form of mild shock that results when fluid and salt are lost through heavy perspiration.

Heat stroke: a life-threatening condition that sets in when heat exhaustion is left untreated and the body has exhausted its efforts to cool itself. Also called sunstroke.

Heat wave: an extended period of high heat and humidity.

Heavy snow: snowfall that reduces visibility to 0.31 mile (0.5 kilometer) and yields, on average, 4 inches (10 centimeters) or more in a twelve-hour period or 6 inches (15 centimeters) or more in a twenty-four-hour period.

Hollow-column: a snowflake in the shape of a long, six-sided column.

Hotshot: a specialized firefighter who ventures into hazardous areas and spends long hours battling blazes.

Hot spot: an area beneath Earth's crust where magma currents rise.

Hurricane: a storm made up of a series of tightly coiled bands of thunderstorm clouds, with a well-defined pattern of rotating winds and maximum sustained winds greater than 74 miles (119 kilometers) per hour.

Hybrid vehicles: vehicles that run on more than one source of power, such as gasoline and electricity.

Hypothermia: a condition characterized by a drop in core body temperature from the normal 98.6°F (37.3°C) to 95°F (35.3°C) or lower.

I

Igneous rock: rock made of solidified molten material that made its way from the interior of the planet to the surface.

Intensity: description of the physical damage caused by an earthquake.

J

Jet stream: the world's fastest upper-air winds. Jet streams travel in a west-to-east direction, at speeds of 80 to 190 miles (130 to 300 kilometers) per hour, around 30,000 feet (9,150 meters) above the ground. Jet streams occur where the largest differences in air temperature and air pressure exist. In North America, jet streams are typically found over southern Canada and the northern United States, as well as over the southern United States and Mexico. The northern jet stream is called the polar jet stream, and the southern jet stream is called the subtropical jet stream.

K

Khamsin: (pronounced kahm-SEEN) a hot, dry, southerly wind that originates on the Sahara and produces large sand and dust storms.

L

La Niña: (pronounced la NEE-nya) a period of unusual cooling of the Pacific Ocean waters off the coast of Peru and Ecuador. It often follows an El Niño.

Lahar: (pronounced LAH-hahr) a mudflow composed of volcanic ash and water that occurs in the wake of a volcanic eruption.

Landslide: the movement of large amounts of soil, rocks, mud, and other debris downward and outward along a slope.

Lava: molten rock that erupts from a fissure or a vent (see magma).

Lava domes: volcanic landmasses with bizarre shapes, made of hardened, thick, layers of lava.

Lava tube: a hollow tube formed when the outer layer of lava is cooled by the air and hardens; molten lava may continue running through the tube.

Leeward: the side of a mountain facing the direction toward which the wind is blowing (in the United States, the eastern side). Cold air descends and produces dry conditions on this side.

Levee: a structure that raises the banks of a river; it increases the channel's water-holding capacity and makes it more difficult for water to overflow onto the surrounding land.

Liquefaction: (pronounced li-quh-FAK-shun) the transformation of water-saturated soil into a liquidlike mass, usually by the action of seismic waves.

Lithosphere: (pronounced LITH-os-fear) the rigid outermost region of Earth, composed of the crust and the upper part of the mantle.

Loose-snow avalanche: avalanche composed of loosely packed snow that begins at a single point and slides down a slope, fanning out in the shape of an inverted "V."

M

Magma: molten rock containing dissolved gas and crystals that originates deep within Earth. When it reaches the surface it is called lava.

Magma chamber: a reservoir of magma beneath Earth's surface.

Magnitude: the power of an earthquake.

Mantle: thick, dense layer of rock that lies beneath Earth's crust. The mantle is about 1,800 miles (2,900 kilometers) thick and accounts for about 84 percent of Earth's volume.

Mesocyclone: region of rotating updrafts created by wind shear within a supercell storm; it may be the beginnings of a tornado.

Meteorite: a chunk of rock and/or metal that breaks off a larger space object, such as an asteroid or a comet, and falls to Earth's surface.

Meteoroid: the term that collectively describes all forms of meteoric material, including meteors and meteorites.

Meteorologist: a scientist who studies weather and climate.

Modified Mercalli Scale: scale developed by Italian seismologist Giuseppe Mercalli to measure the intensity of an earthquake based on the amount of vibration felt by people and the extent of damage to buildings.

Monsoon: seasonal wind that blows from land to sea during the winter and from sea to land during the summer; also, more commonly, a seasonal period of heavy rainfall.

Monsoon climate: a climate that is warm year-round with very rainy (flood-prone) summers and relatively dry winters. It encompasses much of southern and southeastern Asia, the Philippines, coastal regions of northern South America, and slices of central Africa.

Mudflow: a landslide consisting of soil mixed with water. It is wetter than the material in an earthflow.

Multi-vortex tornado: tornado in which the vortex divides into several smaller vortices called suction vortices.

N

NEXRAD: acronym for Next Generation Weather Radar, the network of 156 high-powered Doppler radar units that cover the continental United States, Alaska, Hawaii, Guam, and Korea.

Nor'easter: a strong, northeasterly wind that brings cold air, often accompanied by heavy rain, snow, or sleet, to the coastal areas of New England and the mid-Atlantic states. Also called northeaster.

Numerical prediction model: a computer program that mathematically duplicates conditions in nature. It is often used to predict the weather.

O

Oceanography: the study and exploration of the ocean.

Oxidation: a chemical reaction involving the combination of a material with oxygen.

P

Period: the time between two successive waves.

Pipe: a narrow passageway that leads from a magma reservoir to a vent.

Plate: a large section of Earth's crust.

Plate tectonics: the geologic theory that Earth's crust is composed of rigid plates that "float" toward or away from each other, either directly or indirectly, creating the major geologic features on the planet's surface.

Plinian eruption: a volcanic eruption that releases a deadly cloud of gas, dust, and ash.

Prescribed burn: a planned, controlled fire that clears flammable debris from the forest floor.

Pressure gradient: the rate at which air pressure decreases with horizontal distance.

Pulaski: a combination ax and hoe that is used by firefighters to clear brush and create a fire line. It was invented by forest ranger Edward Pulaski in 1903.

Pumice: volcanic rock formed during the explosive eruption of magma; it has numerous holes produced by gas bubbles and floats on water.

Pyroclastic flow: a rapid flow of hot material consisting of ash, pumice, other rock fragments, and gas ejected by an explosive eruption.

R

Radiosonde: an instrument package carried aloft on a small helium-filled or hydrogen-filled balloon. It measures temperature, air pressure, and relative humidity from the ground to a maximum altitude of about 19 miles (30.4 kilometers) above Earth's surface.

Rain gauge: container that catches rain and measures the amount of rainfall.

Regeneration: the process of making or starting anew.

Richter scale: the scale developed by American seismologist Charles Richter that describes the amount of energy released by an earthquake on a scale from 1 to 10. Each whole number increase in value on the scale indicates a 10-fold increase in the energy released. Earthquakes measuring 7 to 7.9 are major and those measuring 8 or above cause widespread destruction.

Ring of Fire: the name given to the geologically active belt around the Pacific Ocean that is home to more than 75 percent of the world's volcanoes.

River flood: the overflowing of the banks of a river or stream. It may be caused by excessive rain, the springtime melting of snow, blockage of water flow due to ice, or the failure of a dam or aqueduct.

River gauge: a vertical measuring stick immersed in a river to measure changes in water level.

Rockslide: a cascade of rocks (of any size) down a steep slope at high speeds.

S

Saffir-Simpson Hurricane Damage Potential Scale: the scale that ranks hurricanes according to their intensity, using the following criteria: air pressure at the eye of the storm, range of wind speeds, potential height of the storm surge, and the potential damage caused.

Saltation: the wind-driven movement of particles along the ground and through the air.

Saturated: containing the maximum amount of water a material can hold.

Seismic waves: (pronounced SIZE-mic waves) vibrations that move outward from the focus of an earthquake, causing the ground to shake.

Seismograph: an instrument used to detect and measure seismic waves.

Semiarid: a climate in which very little rain or snow falls.

Severe blizzard: a blizzard in which wind speeds exceed 45 miles (72 kilometers) per hour, snowfall is heavy, and the temperature is 10°F (–12°C) or lower.

Severe thunderstorm: a thunderstorm that produces some combination of high winds, hail, flash floods, and tornadoes.

Shamal: (pronounced shah-MALL) a hot, dry, dusty wind that blows for one to five days at a time, producing great dust storms throughout the Persian Gulf.

Shield volcano: a volcano with long, gentle slopes, built primarily by lava flows.

Simoom: (pronounced si-MOOM) a hot, dry, blustery, dust-laden wind that blows across the Sahara and the deserts of Israel, Syria, and the Arabian Peninsula.

Slab avalanche: avalanche that begins when fracture lines develop in a snowpack and a large surface plate breaks away, then crumbles into blocks as it falls down a slope.

Slump: the slow downhill movement of large portions (called blocks) of a slope. Each block rotates backward toward the slope in a series of curving movements.

Solar power: energy, usually in the form of electricity or heat, derived from the Sun's radiation.

Solifluction: (pronounced so-lih-FLUC-shun) the most rapid type of earthflow, occurring when snow or ice thaws or when earthquakes produce shocks that turn the soil into a fluid mass.

Southern Oscillation: shifting patterns of air pressure at sea level, between eastern and western edges of the Pacific Ocean.

Spotting: the starting of new fires, called spot fires, by sparks and embers that drift ahead of an advancing wildfire.

Steam eruption: a violent eruption that occurs when water comes in contact with magma, rapidly turns to steam, and causes the mixture to explode.

Storm surge: a wall of water, usually from the ocean, that sweeps onto shore when the eye of a hurricane passes overhead.

Storm tide: the combined heights of the storm surge and the ocean tide. If a storm surge hits a shore at the same time as a high tide, it can significantly increase the amount of flooding and damage.

Stratus: gloomy, gray, featureless sheets of clouds that cover the entire sky, at low levels of the atmosphere.

Subduction zone: a region where two plates come together and the edge of one plate slides beneath the other.

Suction vortices: small vortices within a single tornado that continually form and dissipate as the tornado moves along, creating the tornado's strongest surface winds.

Supercell storm: the most destructive and long-lasting form of a severe thunderstorm, arising from a single, powerful convective cell. It is characterized by strong tornadoes, heavy rain, and hail the size of golfballs or larger.

Surface fire: a fire with a visible flame that consumes plant material and debris on the forest floor.

T

Tidal station: a floating instrument center in the ocean that records water levels.

Tornadic waterspout: tornado that forms over land and travels over water. Tornadic waterspouts are relatively rare and are the most intense form of waterspouts.

Tornado: rapidly spinning column of air that extends from a thunderstorm cloud to the ground. Also called twister.

Tornado cyclone: spinning column of air that protrudes through the base of a thunderstorm cloud.

Tornado family: a group of tornadoes that develops from a single thunderstorm.

Tornado outbreak: emergence of a tornado family. Tornado outbreaks are responsible for the greatest amount of tornado-related damage.

Trade winds: dominant surface winds near the equator, generally blowing from east to west and toward the equator.

Transpiration: the process by which plants emit water through tiny pores in the underside of their leaves.

Tropical cyclone: any rotating weather system that forms over tropical waters.

Tropical depression: the weakest form of tropical cyclone, characterized by rotating bands of clouds and thunderstorms with maximum sustained winds of 38 miles (61 kilometers) per hour or less.

Tropical disturbance: a cluster of thunderstorms that is beginning to rotate.

Tropical storm: a tropical cyclone weaker than a hurricane, with organized bands of rotating thunderstorms and maximum sustained winds of 39 to 73 miles (63 to 117 kilometers) per hour.

Trough: the lowest point of a wave.

Tsunami: (pronounced tsoo-NAH-mee) a series of giant ocean waves caused by a large displacement of water.

Typhoon: (pronounced TIE-foon) the name for a hurricane that forms over the western North Pacific and China Sea region.

U

Upper-air westerlies: global-scale, upper-air winds that flow in waves heading west to east (but also shifting north and south) through the middle latitudes of the Northern Hemisphere.

Upwelling: the rising up of cold waters from the depths of the ocean, replacing the warm surface water that has moved away horizontally.

V

Vent: an opening in the surface of Earth through which molten rock, lava, ash, and gases escape.

Volcano: an opening in Earth's surface through which gases, hot rocks, and ash are ejected from the heated inner portion of the planet.

Vortex: (plural: vortices) vertical axis of extremely low pressure around which winds rotate.

W

Wall cloud: a roughly circular, rotating cloud that protrudes from the base of a thunderstorm cloud; it is often the beginning of a tornado.

Waterspout: rapidly rotating column of air that forms over a large body of water, extending from the base of a cloud to the surface of the water.

Weather satellite: a satellite equipped with infrared and visible imaging equipment that provides views of storms and continuously monitors weather conditions around the planet.

Whiteout: a condition in which falling, drifting, and blowing snow reduce visibility to almost zero.

Wildfire: a large, uncontrolled fire in grass, brush, or trees.

Windbreak: row of trees or shrubs placed in a farm field to slow the wind and keep it from blowing.

Wind chill factor: the cooling effect on the body due to a combination of wind and temperature.

Wind power: energy, usually in the form of electricity, derived from the wind.

Windward: the side of a mountain facing the direction from which the wind is blowing (in the United States, the western side). Warm air ascends, forms clouds, and yields precipitation on this side.

el niño

El Niño (pronounced el NEE-nyo) is a mass of warm water in the Pacific Ocean that periodically arrives off the coast of South America. The term "el niño" is Spanish for "the child." When it is capitalized as "El Niño," it means "the Christ child." The name was given to this weather phenomenon in the late 1800s by sailors who encountered warm waters off the coast of Peru each year around Christmas time. The term "El Niño" first appeared in print in a Peruvian scientific journal in 1892.

There is evidence that strong El Niños have occurred periodically for thousands of years. In the late 1990s an unusually strong El Niño was blamed for floods, droughts, wildfires, storms, and unseasonable temperatures around the world.

Defining El Niño

Traditionally El Niño has been defined as the annual warming of the waters off the coast of Ecuador and Peru. An enormous pool of warm water—measuring twenty to thirty times the volume of all of the Great Lakes combined—arrives from the western Pacific near the equator, replacing the cold water that usually hugs the South American coast. During most years the warm water only remains for a month or so before the cold water returns.

The temperature of the water off the coast of Peru is usually about 68°F (20°C). When El Niño is present, the water warms—sometimes just barely and other times by several degrees. During the El Niño of December 1997, for example, the water off the coast of Peru warmed to 77°F (25°C).

Words to Know

Air pressure: the pressure exerted by the weight of air over a given area of Earth's surface. Also called atmospheric pressure or barometric pressure.

Convection: the upward motion of a mass of air that has been heated. Convection is the primary way that heat is transferred in the atmosphere. It is the process by which warm air rises up from the ground, to be replaced by cold air. The cold air is then warmed and cycles upward.

Drought: an extended period when the amount of rain or snow that falls on an area is much lower than usual.

Ecosystem: a community of plants and animals, including humans, and their physical surroundings.

El Niño: means "the Christ child" in Spanish. A period of unusual warming of the Pacific Ocean waters off the coast of Peru and Ecuador. It usually starts around Christmas, which is how it got its name.

ENSO: stands for El Niño/Southern Oscillation. It describes the simultaneous warming of the waters in the eastern Pacific Ocean and the shifting pattern of air pressure between the eastern and western edges of the Pacific.

Food chain: transfer of food energy from one organism to another. It begins with a plant species, which is eaten by an animal species; it continues with a second animal species, which eats the first, and so on.

In recent years the term El Niño has come to mean only exceptionally strong El Niño episodes. Such episodes typically take place every three to seven years, but sometimes occur as frequently as every two years or as infrequently as every ten years. During strong El Niño events, coastal water temperatures may rise up to 10°F (5.6°C) above normal. In addition, the warm waters last longer than a few months and spread across much of the eastern Pacific Ocean. The longest recorded El Niño lasted four years, from 1991 through 1995.

Wildfires rage across Southeast Asia

In April 1997 the strongest El Niño in recorded history began. It produced heavy rain and flooding on the Pacific coast of South America, in California, and along the Gulf Coast, as well as in Eastern Europe and in East Africa. Drought and wildfires affected Southeast Asia, Australia, Mexico, Central America, the southern United States, and northeastern Brazil. A series of hurricanes swept through the eastern and

Jet stream: the world's fastest upper-air winds. Jet streams travel in a west-to-east direction, at speeds of 80 to 190 miles (130 to 300 kilometers) per hour, around 30,000 feet (9,150 meters) above the ground. Jet streams occur where the largest differences in air temperature and air pressure exist. In North America, jet streams are typically found over southern Canada and the northern United States, as well as over the southern United States and Mexico. The northern jet stream is called the polar jet stream, and the southern jet stream is called the subtropical jet stream.

La Niña: a period of unusual cooling of the Pacific Ocean waters off the coast of Peru and Ecuador. It often follows an El Niño.

Monsoon: a name for seasonal winds that result in a rainy season occurring in the summer on tropical continents, when the land becomes warmer than the sea beside it.

Numerical prediction model: a computer program that mathematically duplicates conditions in nature. It is often used to predict the weather.

Trade winds: dominant surface winds near the equator, generally blowing from east to west and toward the equator.

Upwelling: the rising up of cold waters from the depths of the ocean, replacing the warm surface water that has moved away horizontally.

western Pacific. By the time the El Niño period ended in May 1998, the unusual weather had killed approximately 23,000 people, and property damage was at least $33 billion.

Southeast Asia had its worst drought in fifty years, which resulted in severe wildfires. Smoke from the fires produced the worst pollution crisis in world history; at least one thousand people died from breathing problems, and hundreds of thousands more were sickened. Scientists estimate that it will take 500 years for the forests on Borneo and Sumatra to recover—assuming they are not further destroyed by fire or logging.

Fires set by landowners

Most of the fires were intentionally set by owners of large rubber, palm oil, timber, and coffee plantations, who use burning as a cheap (although illegal) way to clear forested land for planting. Some of the fires were started by individual farmers who wanted to clear plots of land for growing crops.

In most years, any lingering flames from intentional burns are put out by the annual September monsoon rains. In the El Niño period of 1997–1998, however, the rains did not come. Fire spread rapidly through the parched trees and was propelled by hot winds.

Efforts to stop fire-setting intensified after the 1997–98 fires. In 1999 the Association of South-East Asian Nations (including Indonesia, reportedly the worst fire offender) adopted a policy of "zero-burning." In early 2000, at the start of the dry season, Indonesian government officials viewed satellite images and detected at least 500 fires burning in the Sumatran province of Riau alone. An angry Indonesian environment minister called the fires "a national disaster." That March the government took away the business licenses of four plantation companies accused of setting fires and indicted the companies on charges that could result in huge fines and jail sentences for their top officials. The government also ordered all plantation companies in the area to join forces to put out the fires by the end of March, regardless of who set the fires.

A farmer on the island of Sumatra controls the spread of fire on his land.
REPRODUCED BY PERMISSION OF REUTERS NEWMEDIA INC./CORBIS-BETTMANN.

Orangutans Nearly Driven to Extinction

For the orangutans that inhabit Borneo and Sumatra, the results of the wildfires were disastrous. Thousands of the primates were driven out of the rainforest or killed by the flames. Those orangutans that survived the fire faced starvation due to dwindling food sources. Baby orangutans, too weak to hold onto their mothers, reportedly dropped from trees and died. On Borneo, foresters and environmentalists rescued some 200 orangutans, many of them badly burned, in the first half of 1998.

Prior to the wildfires, orangutans were already considered an endangered species (their population had been reduced by forest clearing and hunting). The effects of the 1997–98 El Niño may have pushed orangutans toward extinction.

Trio of young orangutans. REPRODUCED BY PERMISSION OF W. PERRY CONWAY/CORBIS-BETTMANN.

Effects of the smoke

The smoke throughout Indonesia, Malaysia, and other parts of Southeast Asia was so thick in late 1997 that the sun was blocked for weeks and drivers kept their headlights on during the day. In some parts of Sumatra, visibility was only 2 feet (0.6 meters)—about an arm's length. Schools and businesses were closed, and birds fell from the sky.

In September 1997, poor visibility resulted in an airplane crash in Sumatra that killed 234 people.

The smoke affected about 70 million people throughout Southeast Asia. According to Indonesian news sources, breathing the air during the worst part of the fires was like smoking eighty packs of cigarettes a day. At least 1,000 people died as the result of the smoke, and tens of thousands were sickened. International health experts fear that exposure to the smoke may lead to long-term problems such as cancer, brain damage, reduced life expectancy, and an increase in infant mortality.

Dangerous science: The mechanics of El Niño

In the early 1960s scientists discovered a link between the warming of waters in the eastern Pacific Ocean (El Niño) and a shift in the direction of the major surface winds at the equator—the trade winds. Trade winds originate in the Northern Hemisphere at approximately thirty degrees latitude north (this runs through the southern tip of Florida) and in the Southern Hemisphere at approximately thirty degrees south (this runs through the Amazon jungle region of South America). At those latitudes, air sinks to the surface, warming as it descends, and blows toward the equator. In the Northern Hemisphere trade winds blow to the southwest, and in the Southern Hemisphere trade winds blow to the northwest.

School girls in Indonesia wearing face masks. REPRODUCED BY PERMISSION OF MICHAEL S. YAMASHITA/CORBIS-BETTMANN.

The 1982–1983 El Niño Hits the Western United States

The El Niño of 1982 and 1983 was the second strongest in recorded history (second only to the 1998–99 event). Storms took the lives of more than 2,000 people and caused upwards of $15 billion in damage worldwide. El Niño brought about devastating droughts, floods, and storms on every continent except Antarctica. Damage in the United States was more than $2 billion—almost all of it in the western states.

In early 1983, a string of violent storms traveled across Southern California. The heavy downpours created mudslides and floods. Freeways were submerged, beaches and docks were washed away, and hundreds of homes and businesses were destroyed. A police officer surveying the damage was killed when his helicopter crashed.

Northern California also suffered the ravages of the El Niño induced storms. In Clear Lake, 60 miles north of San Francisco, heavy rains caused a 300-foot wide wall of mud to suddenly slide, crushing a three-year-old boy beneath it. Seven towns in the Sacramento Valley were flooded when the Sacramento River overflowed its banks.

Every so often the trade winds weaken or reverse direction (begin blowing toward the east) in the tropical Pacific Ocean. That change is called the Southern Oscillation (oscillation means shift, swing, or variation). The Southern Oscillation is brought about by a shifting pattern of air pressure between the eastern and western ends of the Pacific Ocean. Air pressure—also known as "barometric pressure" or "atmospheric pressure"—is the weight of the air over a given area. Wind flows from areas of high air pressure to areas of low air pressure, in an attempt to equalize conditions.

As scientists tried to determine the origins of El Niño, they discovered that the arrival of warm water off South America occurs at the same time as the Southern Oscillation. Years marked by El Niño and the Southern Oscillation are called El Niño/Southern Oscillation, or ENSO, years. (They are sometimes called warm-phase ENSO

What Triggers an El Niño?

The mystery of what triggers El Niño has yet to be solved. Scientists have three main theories that might give the answer to this question: undersea volcanic eruptions, sunspots (magnetic storms on the sun's surface), and the previous El Niño.

The first theory is based on the assumption that eruptions and lava leaks from volcanoes on the floor of the eastern Pacific Ocean near South America provide enough heat to warm the water and put an El Niño in motion. This theory is bolstered by the large number of earthquakes that have occurred on the ocean floor, near South America, during recent El Niños. There is a strong correlation between the occurrence of undersea earthquakes and volcanic eruptions (see the chapters on Earthquakes and Volcanoes).

The second theory proposes that El Niño's warming of ocean waters is connected to the cycle of sunspots. Sunspots are areas of magnetic disturbance on the surface of the Sun, sometimes referred to as "storms." When these storms reach maturity they eject plasma (an extremely hot substance made of charged particles) into space. A connection between increased sunspot activity and warmer temperatures on Earth has been established. Scientists are studying the effect of sunspots to determine whether the amount of warming during increased sunspot activity is sufficient to trigger an El Niño.

The third theory is that El Niños occur in cycles, with each successive El Niño being sparked by the one before it. Specifically, as an El Niño weakens, it generates long ocean waves, called Rossby waves, that travel west-

years.) Further study revealed how El Niño and the Southern Oscillation are linked.

Air pressure and water temperature in normal years and ENSO years

In normal (non-El Niño) years, air pressure is higher over the eastern part of the Pacific Ocean, near South America, and lower over the western Pacific, near Australia. This pressure difference causes the trade winds to blow from the higher pressure in the east to the lower pressure in the west, and toward the equator. The winds carry warmth and moisture toward Australia and Indonesia.

ward across the Pacific. The Rossby waves transport the warm surface waters. The warm layer thins near South America, and cold water upwells to take its place. The mass of warm water, driven by westward-blowing trade winds, then piles up in the western Pacific. When the expanse of water in the west becomes so tall (up to 5 feet above sea level) that the trade winds can stack it no higher, the water is drawn down by gravity and flows back to the east—like water sloshing back and forth in a bucket. The shifting position of the warm waters creates a change in the air pressure between one area and another, and the trade winds weaken or reverse direction. The next El Niño is thus set in motion.

None of these theories have been proven yet. Right now they are just "educated guesses" that require additional study.

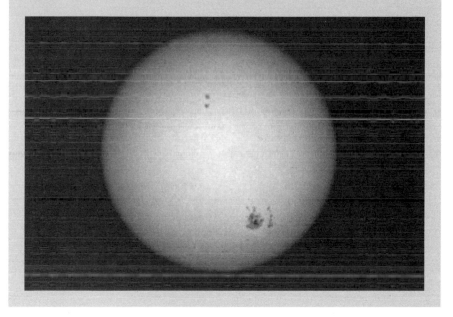

Visible light image of the sun, showing large sunspots. PHOTO COURTESY OF THE U.S. NATIONAL AERONAUTICS AND SPACE ADMINISTRATION.

The trade winds push along the surface of the ocean, forcing warm water to the west and actually increasing the sea level in the western Pacific. This causes the sea level in the eastern Pacific, along the coast of tropical South America, to decrease as the surface layer of warm water is pushed westward. Cold water from the depths of the ocean along the South American coast upwells (rises) to the surface to replace the warmer water that was blown away. As a result, the water in the western Pacific is usually some 14°F (8°C) warmer than the water in the eastern Pacific.

Just prior to an ENSO year, the trade winds grow weaker and sometimes reverse direction, and the warm waters in the western Pacific begin to move toward the east. The air pressure in the eastern Pacific decreases, while the air pressure in the western Pacific rises.

The warm water, which extends for thousands of miles, piles up on the coasts of Peru and Ecuador. As the warm water evaporates into the air and forms clouds, the normally dry coastal South American nations get an above average amount of rainfall—causing flooding and erosion. At the same time, Australia, Indonesia, and the Philippines have unusually dry weather—sometimes causing drought and wildfires.

During a strong ENSO, the warm water flows northward along the west coasts of the Americas, sometimes as far north as northern Canada and Alaska. The moisture and heat from the ocean evaporate into the air, producing clouds and fueling storms that sweep eastward across North America.

Aftermath: Effects of El Niño on the Earth and its inhabitants

With the exception of the changing seasons, El Niño is the single greatest influence upon world weather patterns. El Niño's importance can be understood in terms of the role of oceans in controlling weather and the enormous amount of energy contained in El Niño's warm waters.

Oceans cover more than 70 percent of Earth's surface and are responsible for about one-third of total heat distribution around the planet. It is estimated that the top 10 feet (3 meters) of the ocean water contains as much heat as the entire atmosphere.

The heat that is stored in oceans warms the air just above the ocean's surface. This warm, moist air rises and is blown over land to form clouds. The water vapor within the clouds condenses into droplets and falls to the ground as rain. Because of this process, the world's wettest zones are the regions in which ocean temperatures are highest.

The central Pacific Ocean near the equator, the longest open body of water on Earth, is a tremendous storehouse of heat from the sun. Most of the time, the warmest water is found in a deep layer in the western central Pacific, near Australia and Indonesia. Accordingly, that region has a rainy climate. The waters in the eastern Pacific, off the coast of Peru and Ecuador, are cooler. They put significantly less heat into the air; as a result, comparatively little rain falls in that region.

During El Niño, the pool of warm water moves eastward across the Central Pacific. The result is that the South American coast receives the heavy rains that usually fall in the western Pacific.

El Niño's Sister, La Niña

La Niña (pronounced la NEE-nya) is another type of unusual weather that often follows an El Niño. The term "La Niña" is Spanish for "the girl." It is used to show the close relationship between La Niña and El Niño weather.

The main characteristic of La Niña is a cooling of the waters in the tropical Pacific, from the coast of South America to the central equatorial region. Normally, the temperature of the Pacific Ocean off the coast of South America is around 68°F (20°C). During El Niño years, the water temperature may be up to 10°F (5.6°C) warmer than normal. In contrast, the temperature of coastal waters falls as much as 15°F (8°C) below normal during La Niña years.

In many ways, La Niña's effects on the weather are the opposite of El Niño's. For instance, La Niña brings cold winters to the Pacific Northwest, northern Plains states, Great Lakes states, and Canada, and warmer-than-usual winters to the southeastern states. In addition, El Niño's unruly sister brings drier-than-usual conditions to California, the Southwest, the Gulf of Mexico, and Florida, as well as drought for the South American coast and flooding for the western Pacific region.

A Brazilian woman sits near the ruins of her home after a landslide brought about by torrential La Niña rains wiped out her neighborhood.
REPRODUCED BY PERMISSION OF AFP/CORBIS-BETTMAN.

El Niño, jet streams, and the path of storms

The primary way in which El Niño affects the weather of North America is by altering the position of the jet streams. Jet streams are the world's fastest upper-air winds. They travel from the west to the east at 80 to 190 miles (130 to 300 kilometers) per hour, around 30,000 feet (9,150 meters) or more above the ground.

Jet streams occur where the largest differences in air temperature and air pressure exist. In North America, jet streams are generally found over southern Canada and the northern United States (called the polar front, it's where the cold polar air meets the cool temperate air) and over the southern United States and Mexico (an area known as the subtropics, it's where the cool temperate air meets the warm tropical air). Storms, which are fueled by differences in air temperature, typically travel along the same path as jet streams.

El Niño alters the positions of jet streams with the formation of towering thunderstorms in the eastern Pacific Ocean. During El Niño years, heat and moisture are released into the air over the eastern Pacific and rise in a powerful upward motion (called convection). This process creates towering thunderstorm clouds. The greater the heat and humidity, the taller the clouds and the more intense the thunderstorms.

The towering thunderstorms protrude upward into the jet stream, where they divert the path of high-altitude winds. This process has the consequence of altering the position of storms, and hence the relative wetness and dryness of regions across North America. El Niño affects the path of jet streams and storms in a variety of ways, depending on the strength of the event.

Effects of El Niño on the United States and Canada

In the United States and Canada, El Niño is but one factor among many that contributes to shaping the weather. And the effect of any particular El Niño on the weather depends on the strength of that event—particularly the way in which it affects the positions of the jet streams.

El Niño's influence on the weather is always greatest in the winter. Winter is when El Niño reaches its most mature stage in the Northern Hemisphere. Winter is also when contrasts in temperatures between the northern and southern regions of North America are greatest and when the jet streams are strongest.

During a strong El Niño, the subtropical jet stream strengthens over the southern United States, and sometimes merges with the polar jet stream. The strong subtropical jet stream appears on satellite photos

Why Is a Few Degrees of Warming Such a Big Deal?

You may wonder why the world's weather is so drastically affected by just a few degrees of ocean warming. After all, we experience slight changes in air temperature all the time with little consequence. In the case of El Niño, however, the difference is that the change in temperature occurs in a tremendous mass of water. A temperature increase of even 1°F (0.5°C) throughout such a great mass of water results in a considerable increase in the heat it contains.

Heat is a form of energy. The amount of heat energy contained in a material depends on the mass of the material and its temperature. For example, water is much more dense than air—that is, a bucket filled with water contains much more mass than the same bucket filled with air. As a result, a bucket of warm water contains much more heat energy than a bucket of warm air at the same temperature. Now imagine a bucket so big it covers part of an ocean. That much warm water contains an enormous amount of heat energy—in fact, enough heat energy to significantly change the world's weather. That's what El Niño does.

Just how much heat energy is there in El Niño's warm waters? There is more energy than can be produced in a year by a million 1,000-megawatt power plants; more energy than all the fossil fuel (gasoline, coal, and natural gas) that has burned in the United States since 1900; and as much energy as 500,000 twenty-megaton hydrogen bombs.

as a band of clouds and moisture moving across Mexico and the southern United States. The jet stream brings greater-than-normal rainfall—and in some cases flash floods, mudslides, and tornadoes—to southern California, the southwestern United States, northern Mexico, and the Gulf Coast.

The jet stream may dip south after passing the Gulf Coast. In that case the southeastern United States stays dry, sometimes giving way to wildfires, and has colder-than-usual winters.

Sometimes the polar jet stream meanders farther south than usual and merges with the subtropical jet stream. The polar jet stream typically seals off the cold polar air, keeping it to the north. If it shifts southward, however, it allows cold air to move farther to the south than usual. As a result, southern Canada and the northern United States experience cold, wet weather.

If the jet streams remain apart, the polar jet stream veers north to Alaska before heading eastward across central Canada. In that situation southern Canada and the northern United States remain relatively warm and dry.

During a mild El Niño, a weaker subtropical jet stream traverses Mexico before swinging north over the southeastern United States. In that case the West Coast and Gulf states stay relatively dry—and often experience wildfires—while the southeast gets rain and tornadoes.

The polar jet stream during a mild El Niño heads north into Canada on the western edge of the continent, then dips farther south than usual. With this arrangement the Pacific Northwest stays dry, while the states in the Midwest and northeast, as well as southern Canada, have cold, wet weather, and sometimes flooding.

The warm waters of El Niño also fuel the development of hurricanes in the equatorial eastern Pacific. Occasionally those hurricanes travel north and soak the coast of southern California, eastward to Texas.

Effects of El Niño on South America and the Caribbean

El Niño's effect is experienced most directly on the west coast of South America, particularly in Peru and Ecuador. There the warming of the water disrupts the fishing-based economy. Under normal conditions, cold water, rich in nutrients, rises up from the depths of the ocean to the surface along the shore. The cold water contains phosphates and nitrates that sustain tiny marine plants called phytoplankton (pronounced FIE-toe-plank-ton). The phytoplankton are eaten by tiny marine animals called zooplankton. The zooplankton, in turn, are food for fish. Under El Niño conditions, warm water replaces the cold water. The warm water holds few nutrients; it is inhospitable to phytoplankton and, as a result, to zooplankton and fish. When the coastal water is warm, large numbers of fish die off or migrate in search of food.

While El Niño brings hard times to fishermen in Peru and Ecuador, it is a blessing to coastal farmers. The warm water fuels intense storms that irrigate dry cropland. To the farmers of western Peru and Ecuador, El Niño years are known as *años de abundancia* (years of abundance in Spanish). In some years, however, El Niño-induced rain causes flash floods that wash away homes and destroy fields.

In the west-central portion of the continent—Chile, Paraguay, and Argentina, in particular—El Niño brings excess rain to normally dry regions (much of it desert). That precipitation that falls in the mountains runs down the slopes and floods low-lying cities. In Chile's Ataca-

An aerial view shows the cultivated fields of a valley in the Atacama Desert, Chile, during an El Niño year. REPRODUCED BY PERMISSION OF GALEN ROWELL/CORBIS-BETTMANN.

Brazil Suffers Drought and Famine

Northeast Brazil was hard-hit by El Niño-induced droughts that intensified in 1983, and again in 1998. In the former case, 88 percent of the poverty-ridden region was beset by a lack of rainfall. Some 14 million subsistence farmers were plunged into debt by crop losses. Making matters worse, the price of food tripled.

During the 1998 El Niño, northeast Brazil suffered its worst drought of the century. The dryness was so intense that the rain forest went up in flames. Agricultural yields were far lower than normal and a famine beset the region. Nine-and-a-half million people were at risk of starvation. Many people left their farms and villages for lack of food and water and moved to the outskirts of big cities.

Hungry subsistence farmers organized to demand fairness in food distribution and government assistance. Led by the Landless Workers' Movement (known by the initials MST for its name in Portuguese)—an organization promoting redistribution of land from the wealthiest one percent of Brazilians, who hold almost half of all farmland, to landless peasants—the farmers raided food trucks and warehouses and looted supermarkets. At least 110 food raids took place in the first half of 1998.

In response to the problem, Brazilian President Fernando Henrique Cardoso announced a $500 million relief program. The relief measures included food distribution, a work-relief program, an irrigation system in drought-prone areas, and job training and literacy initiatives.

ma Desert, one of the driest places in the world (sometimes going twenty years without a drop of rain), El Niño can bring enough rain to make wildflowers bloom and roads flood. El Niño also brings heavier-than-usual rainfall to Uruguay and southern Brazil.

During El Niño, the northeastern portion of Brazil, as well as Central America, the Caribbean, and southern Mexico typically suffer drought. In some cases crop yields in the region are reduced so drastically that the local population goes hungry. The dry weather also increases the likelihood of forest fires.

The west coast of Mexico, in contrast to the inland portion of the country, experiences storms and Pacific hurricanes fueled by El Niño's warm waters.

El Niño Weather Around the World

Below is a summary of El Niño-inspired weather patterns around the world. This information represents general trends, not rules. It is even possible that the weather in a given location during a particular El Niño may be the opposite of what is listed below. During El Niño years, weather patterns are influenced not only by the strength of the event but also a host of other factors.

- Increased precipitation and flooding in Peru, Ecuador, Chile, Paraguay, Argentina, Uruguay, southern Brazil, California and Arizona eastward through the southern United States, east-central Africa, central and eastern Europe, and western Australia.

- Drought in Northeastern Brazil, Central America, the Caribbean, southern Mexico, Australia (except the west coast), India, southeast Asia, Papua New Guinea, California (during weak El Niño), and southern Africa.

- Increased hurricane activity in the west coast of Mexico, southern California to Texas, Asia (along the coast of Indian Ocean), and Madagascar.

- Warmer than usual winter in the northern United States, western Canada, Alaska, northern Europe, southeast Asia, Japan, North Korea, South Korea, Mongolia, southeast Australia, and southeast Africa.

- Colder than usual winter in the southeastern United States.

Effects of El Niño on Africa, Asia, Australia, and Europe

El Niño brings dry conditions—and often droughts and wildfires—to Australia, Southeast Asia, India, and Africa. In recent years, the worst El Niño-induced droughts occurred in Australia, India, Papua New Guinea, southeast Asia, and southern Africa. Wildfires raged out of control in Australia, Indonesia, and Malaysia (see section "Wildfires Rage Across Southeast Asia" on page 138). El Niño is unpredictable in eastern Africa; it sometimes brings drought and other times flooding. Central and eastern Europe sometimes experience excessively rainy weather during El Niño.

El Niño encourages the development of hurricanes in the Pacific Ocean (or cyclones, as they are called in the western Pacific region) and typhoons (another regional word for hurricanes) in the Indian Ocean. During El Niño years, hurricanes and tropical storms (storm systems that form in the tropics and that are weaker than hurricanes) dump heavy rains throughout much of Asia.

Effects of El Niño on animal life

El Niño not only causes severe weather problems, but it also spells disaster for many types of marine life and land animals. As previously explained, the warm waters of El Niño do not support phytoplankton and zooplankton. Fish, which feed on plankton, either move to colder waters or starve.

The effects of the lack of fish are felt all the way up the food chain and last for several years. Marine birds and marine mammals (such as sea lions) that feed on fish throughout the Pacific Ocean region face starvation. Animals that prey upon sea birds also decline in number.

El Niño weather also endangers animal life as a result of river flooding, which places sediments and contaminants into coastal waters; large ocean waves, which erode seashore habitats; and forest fires in drought-plagued regions, which drive wildlife from their homes.

Sea birds. In El Niño years sea birds, primarily terns and gulls, are the animals most directly affected by the shortage of fish. Sea birds in the western Pacific have difficulty finding enough food for themselves and their chicks.

One of the worst El Niños for sea birds was in 1957–58. During that time some 18 million birds off the coast of Peru perished. Cormorants, boobies, and pelicans were among the hardest-hit species. The 1982–83 El Niño was also particularly rough on sea birds: 85 percent of the population off the coast of Peru died or migrated in search of food. The 17 million sea birds inhabiting Christmas Island (in the middle of the Pacific Ocean) also abandoned their homes at that time.

The decline of least terns in California during the El Niño of 1982–83 is of particular interest to scientists. The fish that terns usually feed on were few in number and small in size. Female terns laid their eggs later than usual and the eggs were abnormally small. Many females abandoned their nests for lack of food and many of the chicks that did hatch did not develop properly. Large numbers of the weakened chicks were preyed upon by small hawks called American kestrels.

It was not until 1988 that the California least tern colony recovered. The consequences of the 1982–83 El Niño were felt for so long, in part, because least terns do not breed until they are two or three years old. Thus, in 1984 and 1985 the number of breeding terns was smaller than usual.

The sea bird population was reduced again during the 1997–98 El Niño. Albatrosses in the Galápagos Islands abandoned their nests for colder waters. Peru's populations of Inca tern, guanay, and red-legged cormorant also suffered declines.

Also during the 1997–98 El Niño, the brown pelican population in Baja California and the Gulf of California (on Mexico's west coast) fell to its lowest level in thirty years. During normal years there are between 10,000 and 20,000 nests in the brown pelican colony; in March and April 1998, researchers found only 280 nests. Just one month later, not a single nest could be found. Biologists predicted that the pelican population would recover once the waters cooled and the anchovies, herrings, and sardines returned.

Sea mammals. Populations of sea lions, fur seals, and other sea mammals are also reduced during El Niño years. Those animals, which live in colonies along the South American and California coasts and on the

Dead pelicans and sea lions on the beach near Paracas, Peru, in 1998.

Galápagos Islands (west of Ecuador), subsist mainly on anchovies. The shortage of anchovies (and secondary food sources halibut, lanternfish, rockfish, and squid) during El Niño years takes the greatest toll on young animals. Seal and sea lion pups go hungry because their mothers spend much more time than usual (five to six days, instead of the typical one to two days) seeking fish rather than nursing their young. Pups either starve or grow weak. Many of the pups that survive their first season later prove incapable of feeding themselves, and perish.

During the 1982–83 El Niño, 90 percent of the fur seal pups in Peru died. In the same season, more than half of the elephant seal pups in California were killed in storms that flooded beaches where seals are born.

Seal colonies on the California coast were especially hard hit during the 1997–98 El Niño. More than 6,000 pups in a colony on San Miguel island had perished by the end of 1997. The mortality rate of the pups climbed to 70 percent; in normal years just 25 percent of the young animals die.

At El Niño's peak in early 1998, the temperature of the water off Peru's Paracas Peninsula, which is normally 56 to 58°F (13 to 14°C), measured 81 to 83°F (27 to 28°C). The results of this extreme warming could be seen in the thousands of sea lion and seal carcasses littering South American beaches from Chile to Ecuador.

Galápagos Islands iguanas and penguins. Another organism that cannot survive in the warm El Niño waters is green algae (pronounced

Fishermen load anchovies onto their boat off the coast of Peru.
REPRODUCED BY PERMISSION OF BATES LITTLEHALES/CORBIS-BETTMANN.

AL-gee). Green algae, which thrive in cold water, are the main food source of the marine iguana—a 39-inch- (1-meter-) long reptile that lives on the Galápagos Islands. When the water heats up, the green algae become stunted. Brown algae, which do thrive in warm water but are not digestible by marine iguanas, form a layered coating on the green algae. During the 1982–83 El Niño, as the green algae declined, much of the Galápagos marine iguana population was wiped out. In 1998, when the waters warmed by 10°F (5.6°C), marine iguanas suffered again.

The penguins that live on the Galápagos Islands also bear the brunt of El Niño. Galápagos penguins live on several of the islands, including the northernmost islands that are north of the equator. That makes these flightless birds, which measure 20 to 24 inches (0.5 to 0.6 meters) high and weigh 4 to 5 pounds (1.8 to 2.3 kilograms), the only penguin species naturally occurring in the Northern Hemisphere.

The staple of the penguins' diet is small fish, primarily mullet, which leave the vicinity of the islands to escape the warm El Niño waters. Since penguins live primarily on land, and the nearest land is 600 miles (960 kilometers) away, they are unable to migrate in search of food. During the 1998 El Niño researchers observed starving adult penguins and no juveniles—suggesting either that the birds did not breed or, if they did breed, all of the chicks died.

In the aftermath of the El Niño of 1997–98, the Galápagos penguin population numbered less than 8,500—less than half of its 1970 size.

Effects of El Niño on human health

The unusual weather of El Niño affects the health of human beings in many ways. For instance, hunger is a problem in areas where crops die due to drought. Respiratory ailments flare up in regions ravaged by forest fires. And many diseases are spread by organisms that reproduce rapidly during El Niño years.

Cholera, dysentery, and typhoid are diseases that typically spread during floods, when sewage treatment systems become overloaded and drinking water supplies become contaminated. An abundance of standing water also promotes the breeding of mosquitoes, which may carry malaria, dengue fever, yellow fever, and encephalitis (pronounced EN-cef-a-LIE-tis).

During the 1982–83 El Niño, flooding in Ecuador, Bolivia, Colombia, Peru, India, and Sri Lanka resulted in epidemics of malaria. And in early 1998, a malaria outbreak came to Peru due to El Niño-induced flooding. In the Piura region of northwest Peru, home to 1.5 million people, there were some 30,000 cases of the disease.

El Niño Bleaches Coral Reefs

Coral reefs, which are undersea ecosystems sometimes referred to as the "rainforests of the oceans," are among the most species-rich places on Earth. Coral reefs are colonies of coral polyps (pronounced PALL-ups)—small, tube-shaped animals with hard exterior skeletons coated with colorful algae. The algae, which give the coral reefs the appearance of underwater gardens, are essential to the survival of the polyps.

Coral reefs are found in the warm, shallow waters of tropical oceans and can survive only within a small temperature range. An increase in temperature of just a few degrees can kill the algae. When the algae die, the coral bleaches (turns a whitish color). Bleaching typically leads to the death of a polyp colony.

Many coral reefs were bleached during the 1982–83 El Niño, when eastern Pacific Ocean temperatures increased by 4 to 5°F (2 to 3°C). Some coral species were wiped out entirely. The most extensive damage to coral reefs occurred off the coasts of the Galápagos Islands, Ecuador, Colombia, Panama, and Costa Rica. There the losses to 300-year-old coral reefs ranged from 50 to 97 percent. Scientists estimate that it will take centuries for the corals in those areas to recover.

The bleaching of corals recurred during the 1997–98 El Niño. Significant damage was done to the reefs off the Pacific coasts of Panama, Costa Rica, and Mexico. The warm waters also wiped out an 18-mile- (29-kilometer-) long coral colony along the Great Barrier Reef of Australia. Varying degrees of bleaching also occurred in coral reefs off the coasts of French Polynesia, Kenya, the Galápagos Islands, the Florida Keys, Baja California, Mexico's Yucatan coast, the Cayman Islands, and the Netherland Antilles. The corals at most of these sites were expected to recover once the water temperature returned to normal.

Also in 1983, the unusually mild and moist spring and summer in California gave rise to record numbers of fleas carrying the bubonic plague, an infectious disease that wiped out one-fourth of Europe's population during the Middle Ages (476–1453). Fleas spread the disease to mammals, which can pass on the illness to humans. In 1983, thirty-six people contracted the plague (all in western states), and six of them died. That outbreak was the most severe in the United States since the 1920s.

In 1993 El Niño conditions led to an outbreak of a deadly disease in the southwestern United States. The disease, caused by a type of virus called hantavirus, killed several people in the Four Corners region (where Arizona, Utah, Colorado, and New Mexico converge).

The hantavirus is carried by desert-dwelling rodents called deer mice. In normal years, the deer mouse population is relatively small—their numbers are kept in check by a limited food supply and the presence of predators (such as owls and snakes). During the 1992 El Niño, however, the desert in the Four Corners region received a lion's share of rain. Plant life exploded, as did the deer mouse population.

Along with the greater numbers of deer mice came increased deer mouse droppings. People who either touched the droppings or breathed dust contaminated with the droppings risked exposure to the hantavirus. When the rains stopped and the desert returned to its arid state, the hantavirus outbreak subsided.

The human factor: A possible connection between global warming and El Niño

The strongest El Niños on record occurred in the 1980s and 1990s. That reality has prompted scientists to consider whether human activity—namely global warming—has an effect on El Niño (also see the chapter on Global Warming).

Global warming is the theory that the average temperatures around the world have begun to rise, and will continue to rise, because of an increase of certain gases in Earth's atmosphere. These gases are called "greenhouse gases" because they let sunlight come in, but don't let heat go back out into space—as if Earth was covered with a big glass greenhouse that keeps everything warm. The most plentiful greenhouse gases are water vapor and carbon dioxide. Other greenhouse gases include methane, nitrous oxide, and chlorofluorocarbons.

The increase of carbon dioxide in the atmosphere is believed to be the main reason for global warming. Carbon dioxide is produced by burning fossil fuels—such as coal, fuel oil, gasoline, and natural gas—and is emitted into the air by homes, factories, and motorized vehicles. During the last century, the amount of carbon dioxide in the atmosphere increased by 30 percent. During that same period, the average air temperature increased slightly more than 1°F (0.5°C). The warmest year in U.S. history was 1998, and the warmest two years in the world since accurate record-keeping began in 1880 were 1997 and 1998.

Flooding and Mudslides in Peru and Ecuador

South America received unusually large amounts of rain and snow during the El Niño of 1997–98. Chile reported ten times its normal amount of rain for the period. Floods and mudslides damaged crops, buildings, roads, and bridges. In Chile's Atacama Desert, one of the driest places in the world, heavy rains washed out roads. Rain drenched the central Andes and rolled down the mountainsides, causing serious flooding in Chile's capital city, Santiago. Paraguay, Uruguay, northeastern Argentina, and southern Brazil also experienced heavy rains that damaged buildings and crops.

During the same period, Peru and Ecuador suffered storms, floods, and mudslides that claimed 450 lives and created more than $3 billion in damage to crops, roads, and buildings. In coastal Peru storms washed away some 300,000 homes, downed electric power lines, and destroyed roads and bridges. Water-borne diseases such as cholera and hepatitis, and mosquito-transmitted diseases such as malaria and dengue fever, spread quickly in coastal Peru.

Heavy snowstorms in the Peruvian Andes caused the deaths of 2,500 cold-weather, llama-like animals called alpacas. In Peru's coastal Sechura Desert, which is usually so dry that the ground is hard and cracked, flood waters formed a lake 90 miles (145 kilometers) long, 20 miles (32 kilometers) wide, and 10 feet (3 meters) deep—the largest lake in Peru. Government officials stocked the temporary lake with fish to ease food shortages.

According to a group of the world's leading weather scientists, humans are having an effect on the weather. The question remains: Is that human influence affecting El Niño?

Arguments for and against the global warming connection

One theory about the connection between global warming and increased El Niño activity is as follows: As the planet warms, heat builds up in the Pacific Ocean. El Niño acts as an escape valve for the excess heat, moving it eastward across the ocean and then releasing it into the atmosphere. Furthermore, computer simulations (computer programs that mimic real-world events) show that increased carbon dioxide levels in the atmosphere lead to an uneven heating of the planet. In the Pacific Ocean, according to the simulation, the eastern portion warms to a greater degree than the western portion—exactly the conditions found during El Niño.

A massive flood
washes away a
cemetery in Peru in
1998. REPRODUCED BY
PERMISSION OF ARCHIVE
PHOTOS, INC.

While many scientists believe that global warming may affect El Niño, few believe that is the entire reason. El Niño experts point out that huge shifts have occurred in the global climate over the past hundreds of thousands of years, without any human influence such as global warming. Natural variability in climate has ranged from ice ages to warm periods. And at certain times in our planet's past, El Niño-like conditions have lasted for thousands of years.

Many scientists refuse to make conclusions about the impact of global warming on El Niño based on one century's worth of data. Those scientists argue that at least another century of careful measurement of El Niños is needed to make such a determination.

Technology connection: Predicting El Niño

In recent years scientists have developed the tools to make predictions about the development, intensity, and effects of El Niño. They use a combination of computer models and measurements of air and water conditions in the tropical Pacific Ocean. The measurements are taken by a network of weather buoys (drifting or anchored floating objects containing weather instruments) and satellites, supplemented by readings taken on ships. With today's technology, meteorologists (scientists who study weather and climate) at weather prediction centers are able to observe changes in the ocean as they occur.

Prediction capabilities have vastly improved since the strong El Niño of 1982–83. Meteorologists, for the first time, successfully anticipated the 1997–98 El Niño several months before it occurred.

El Niño predictions remain of a general nature, such as whether conditions in a given region will be wetter, drier, colder, or warmer than usual. Crop growing season forecasts issued by international climate prediction agencies declare one of the following: near-normal conditions; a weak El Niño with a slightly wetter than normal growing season; a full-blown El Niño with flooding; or cooler than normal waters offshore, with a higher than normal chance of drought (in other words, La Niña).

Computer-based prediction

Since the early 1980s, meteorologists have used computer models of climate change (also called climate modeling) in their efforts to predict El Niños. Climate modeling relies on a sophisticated computer program, called a numerical prediction model. The model incorporates mathematical equations that mimic processes in nature. The equations are based on the laws of oceanic and atmospheric physics, which describe motion, thermodynamics (the relationship between heat and mechanical energy), and the behavior of water.

When a set of data describing current conditions is entered into the computer, the program predicts what is likely to happen several months in the future. The computer models are constantly updated with data from the weather buoys and satellites.

Tropical Ocean-Global Atmosphere (TOGA)

In the early 1980s, officials of the World Meteorological Organization (a Geneva, Switzerland-based agency of the United Nations) developed an ocean-monitoring system called the Tropical Ocean-Global Atmosphere (TOGA). The stated purpose of TOGA was: "to explore the predictability of the tropical ocean-atmosphere system and the impact on the global atmospheric climate on time scales of months to years." The implementation of TOGA was hastened by the strong 1982–83 El Niño— the episode that got underway during the planning stages of TOGA.

TOGA was managed by the National Oceanic and Atmospheric Administration (NOAA) of the United States and weather agencies of France, Japan, Korea, and Taiwan, with the cooperation of thirteen other nations. The program operated from 1985 to 1994. During that period TOGA researchers observed interactions between the air and sea in the equatorial Pacific and determined how those interactions would affect climate change around the world.

Scientist adjusting sensors on TOGA-TAO buoy. REPRODUCED BY PERMISSION OF THE NATIONAL OCEANIC AND ATMOSPHERIC ADMINISTRATION.

TOGA collected data with weather buoys, satellites, ships, and tidal gauges (instruments that measure the comings and goings of the tides). The instruments, collectively, measured water temperature at the ocean surface and to a depth of 1,650 feet (500 meters), as well as air temperature, relative humidity, ocean currents, sea level, and the speed and direction of surface winds. All data was sent daily, via satellite, to weather prediction centers.

Some of the weather buoys were drifting and others were moored (anchored to the ocean floor). The drifting buoys sent signals that indicated their positions, and thus told the direction of surface water motion. The drifters also recorded air pressure and temperature of surface ocean water at various locations. The moored buoys measured surface winds and temperatures at different ocean depths.

The information collected by TOGA added to scientists' understanding of El Niño's life cycle. The program also provided the first means of monitoring the Pacific Ocean and the atmosphere in real-time (as it occurs).

Tropical Atmosphere Ocean Array (TAO)

The TOGA program ended in 1994. However, it resulted in the establishment of a permanent, international network of ocean-atmosphere monitoring. That system, which uses moored and drifting buoys, satellites, and research ships, is called the El Niño-Southern Oscillation Monitoring System.

The most important element of the monitoring system is the Tropical Atmosphere Ocean Array (TAO). The TAO array, which was completed in December 1994 as TOGA was coming to an end, takes continuous ocean measurements. Its purpose is to detect El Niños in their earliest stages and improve forecasting. The TAO project is jointly coordinated by the NOAA and weather agencies in Japan, Taiwan, and France. It is headquartered at the NOAA's Pacific Marine Environmental Laboratory (PMEL) in Seattle, Washington.

The TAO array consists of sixty-five moored buoys and five current meters (instruments that measure the strength and direction of currents), spanning the equatorial Pacific. The buoys and meters are stationed at intervals between longitudes of 135 degrees east (near Indonesia) and 95 degrees west (just west of Peru), and latitudes 10 degrees north and 10 degrees south (forming a wide band with the equator in the center). They stretch across one-third of the Earth's circumference. (Degrees of longitude are imaginary lines encircling the Earth, perpendicular to the equator, that tell one's position east or west

TAO Predicts 1997–98 El Niño

The 1997-98 El Niño was the first such episode to be successfully predicted months ahead of time. In December 1996, the TAO staff noticed that the trade winds had weakened and issued the prediction that El Niño was coming. An eastward movement of warm ocean surface waters was detected in early 1997, supporting that prediction.

Fifteen years earlier, when a strong El Niño had been developing, forecasters had entirely missed the warning signs. The 1982–83 event occurred just prior to the placement of weather buoys across the Pacific. At that time researchers relied mainly on satellite readings of sea level (from which they were able to determine temperature) for clues to El Niño. Those readings were altered by the April 1982 volcanic eruption of El Chichon in Mexico. The soot and ash, which had spewed high into the air during the eruption, clouded the satellites' vision and masked the rising sea level in the eastern Pacific. Since that time researchers have developed methods of adjusting satellite measurements to account for volcanic eruptions.

on the globe; degrees of latitude run parallel to the equator and tell one's position north or south on the globe.)

The buoys of TAO measure air temperature, surface wind speed and direction, relative humidity, sea surface temperature, and ocean temperature to a depth of 1,650 feet (500 meters). The buoys and current meters transmit information, via NOAA satellites, continuously to TAO project headquarters. The data is entered into high-speed computers and analyzed, after which it is sent to weather prediction centers and climate researchers around the world.

TAO's computers combine the thousands of continuous readings from the buoys into a single picture. That picture appears on researchers' monitors as a checkerboard with different colored squares. The color of each square indicates the instruments' readings of ocean and atmosphere at a given location. Several times a day new readings are entered and the picture is updated. In that way it is possible to view a series of pictures in rapid succession—like a movie of ocean conditions. Through this process researchers can literally watch El Niños unfold.

A matter of survival: Using predictions to prepare for El Niño

With advance warning of the destructive weather El Niño has in store, societies can make preparations to minimize the damage. El Niño predictions are most valuable to people involved in agriculture and fishing, especially in tropical nations. (The tropics generally suffer the greatest consequences of El Niño's droughts and flooding.) Other areas in which El Niño predictions are useful are public health, transportation, forestry, water resources, and energy production.

Peru, Australia, Brazil, Ethiopia, and India have all used El Niño predictions to manage agriculture. Farmers in these countries consider the expected precipitation levels and temperature when deciding which crops, and how much of each crop, to plant.

One example of the rewards reaped from an El Niño prediction is the improvement in northeastern Brazilian agricultural yields in 1991 over those of 1987. In a typical year, farmers in the state of Ceara in northeastern Brazil produce 716,000 tons (644,400 metric tons) of rice, beans, and corn. In 1987 the region experienced an El Niño-related drought, and crop production fell to 110,000 tons (99,000 metric tons). In 1991, in contrast, farmers heeded warnings of a coming El Niño. Government agencies provided farmers with seeds that were drought-resistant and had shorter growing seasons. As a result, 584,000 tons (525,600 metric tons) of crops were harvested—five times as much as in the previous drought.

Farmers and fishermen in northern Peru benefited from predictions issued in advance of the 1997–98 El Niño. Anticipating heavy rains and the sprouting of grass on normally dry land, farmers raised cattle. Farmers also planted rice—a crop that does well in wet conditions. (During dry years, in contrast, farmers may plant cotton—a crop that requires little rain.) Fishermen planned for a harvest of shrimp, since those marine animals inhabit the warm waters that El Niño brings.

If governments are aware that El Niño conditions will contribute to crop losses or shortages of drinking water, they may stockpile food and water for their citizens. In addition, health precautions may be taken in areas where flooding is expected to induce outbreaks of water-borne or mosquito-borne diseases.

El Niño predictions are also helpful in reducing the damage caused by high waves and flooding along the west coasts of South and North America. With advance warning, residents may build barriers to prevent beach erosion, construct storm drains, and reinforce bridges and other structures. At the same time, they may halt new construction projects.

For more information

Books

Arnold, Caroline. *El Niño: Stormy Weather for People and Wildlife*. New York: Clarion Books, 1998.

Fagan, Brian. *Floods, Famines and Emperors: El Niño and the Fate of Civilizations*. New York: Basic Books, 1999.

Glantz, Michael H. *Currents of Change: El Niño's Impact on Climate and Society*. New York: Cambridge University Press, 1996.

Glynn, P. W., ed. *Global Ecological Consequences of the 1982–83 El Niño-Southern Oscillation*. Amsterdam: Elsevier Science Publishers, 1990.

Periodicals

Bond, Kathleen. "Church Backs Poor in Drought; Brazil's Leaders Slow to Respond." *National Catholic Reporter*. (August 14, 1998): p. 11+.

Brownlee, Shannon, and Laura Tangley. "The Wrath of El Niño." *U.S. News and World Report*. (October 6, 1997).

"California Communities Hardest Hit by Week-Long Storm." U.P.I. (March 3, 1983).

Chang, Maria L. "Rain Forests, Forests on Fire." *Science World*. (April 13, 1998). p. 6.

Coles, Peter. "All Eyes on El Niño." *UNESCO Courier*. (May 1999): p. 30.

Cutlip, Kimbra. "El Niño 1997–98: Changing the Way We Think About the Weather." *Weatherwise*. (March/April 1998): pp. 12–13.

Doubilet, David. "Galápagos Underwater." *National Geographic*. (April 1999): pp. 32–40.

"Fire and Rain." *Time International*. (April 20, 1998): p. 34+.

Hart, Daniela. "Northeast Brazil Faces Famine from Drought." *The Washington Post*. (May 17, 1998): p. A26.

Hayden, Thomas. "Enter La Niña, Smiling." *Newsweek*. (December 14, 1998): p. 59.

Helvarg, David. "Weathering El Niño: Hardest Hit and Perhaps the Most Overlooked, the World's Forests Could Feel the Effects for Generations." *American Forests*. (Autumn 1998): p. 29+.

Hudson, Michael. "California Weather." U.P.I. (January 26, 1983)

Johnson, Tim. "Battered by El Niño, South American Sea Lions and Seals Succumb to Hunger." *The Miami Herald*. (July 28, 1998).

Koop, David. "Wild Child: Although It's Called a Child, 'El Niño' Threatens to Severely Disrupt Weather Patterns." *The Ann Arbor News (A.P.)*. (June 1997): pp. D1–D2.

Le Comte, Douglas. "Weather Around the World: A Year of Epic Disasters." *Weatherwise*. (March/April 1998): pp. 29–33.

———. "Weather Highlights Around the World: 1997." *Weatherwise*. (March/April 1998): pp. 26–31.

———. "The Weather of 1998: A Wet and Stormy Year." *Weatherwise.* (March/April 1998): pp. 14–21.

Linden, Eugene. "Smoke Signals: Vast Forest Fires Have Scarred the Globe, but the Worst May Be Yet to Come." *Time.* (June 22, 1998): p. 50+.

Matthews, Jay. "Plague-Infected Squirrel Is Found in Los Angeles." *The Washington Post.* (October 7, 1983): p. A1.

Mazza, Patrick. "The Invisible Hand: As Human Activity Warms the Earth, El Niño Grows More Violent." *Sierra.* (May-June 1998): p. 68+.

Mydans, Seth. "Southeast Asia Chokes on Indonesia's Forest Fires." *The New York Times.* (September 25, 1997): pp. A1, A14.

Nash, J. Madeleine. "Floods and Fires? They're Just the Beginning of El Niño's Impact." *Time.* (June 1, 1998): p. 26.

Ocko, Stephanie. "Sea Change: The Birth of an El Niño." *Weatherwise.* (December 1997): p. 16.

"Operation Rescue." *Time.* (June 1, 1998): p. 26.

Rauss, Uli. "After the Fires." *World Press Review.* (March 1998): p. 39.

Shabe, John. "The Good, the Bad, the Soggy." *Contact Kids.* (November 1998): p. 8.

Suplee, Curt. "El Niño/La Niña: Nature's Vicious Cycle." *National Geographic.* (March 1999): pp. 72–95.

"That Dreadful Smog Is Back." *The Economist.* (March 18, 2000): p. 40.

"When the Smoke Clears in Asia." *The Economist.* (October 4, 1997): p. 43+.

Zimmer, Carl. "The El Niño Factor." *Discover.* (January 1999): pp. 98–106.

Web sites

"The Borneo Project." *Earth Island Institute.* [Online] http://www.earthisland. org/borneo/ (accessed on March 8, 2001) .

"El Niño and Climate Prediction." *National Oceanic and Atmospheric Administration.* [Online] http://www.pmel.noaa.gov/toga-tao/el-nino-report.html (accessed on March 8, 2001).

"El Niño-Southern Oscillation Page." *National Oceanic and Atmospheric Administration.* [Online] http://www.elnino.noaa.gov/ (accessed on March 8, 2001).

"El Niño Special Report." *Environmental News Network.* [Online] http://www.enn. com/specialreports/elnino/ (accessed on March 8, 2001).

"ENSO." *The Weather Channel.* http://www.weather.com/encyclopedia (accessed on March 8, 2001).

Hoover, Mark. "El Niño Scorecard." *NOVA Online.* [Online] http://www.pbs.org/ wgbh/nova/elnino/now/scorecard.html (accessed on March 8, 2001).

"Impacts of El Niño and Benefits of El Niño Prediction." *National Oceanic and Atmospheric Administration.* [Online] http://www.pmel.noaa.gov/toga-tao/el-nino/ impacts.html (accessed on March 8, 2001).

"NOAA El Niño Page." *National Oceanic and Atmospheric Administration* [Online] http://www.elnino.noaa.gov/ (accessed on March 8, 2001).

"Real-Time Monitoring of the ENSO Cycle." *National Oceanic and Atmospheric Administration.* [Online] http://www.pmel.noaa.gov/tao/ (accessed on March 8, 2001).

"Tracking El Niño." *NOVA Online.* [Online] http://www.pbs.org/wgbh/nova/elnino (accessed on March 8, 2001).

"Understanding El Niño and La Niña." *USA Today Climate Science.* [Online] http://www.usatoday.com/weather/nino/wnino0.htm (accessed on March 8, 2001).

"What Is an El Niño?" *National Oceanic and Atmospheric Administration.* [Online] http://www.pmel.noaa.gov/toga-tao/el-nino-story.html (accessed on March 8, 2001).

A flood is the overflow of water onto land that is normally dry. Flooding occurs when the water level rises and overflows the banks of a river or some other low-lying channel, or when high ocean waters wash over the coast. In many parts of the world, floods happen frequently. While flooding is a disaster in many cases, in other cases floods are relied upon to replenish nutrients in the soil and to sustain crops.

Worldwide, 40 percent of all deaths from natural disasters are due to floods. Floods, and flash floods in particular, kill more people than any other weather phenomenon. In the United States, there are about 140 deaths per year due to floods—the majority of those occur in flash floods.

A flash flood is a sudden, violent flood. It is caused by persistent, heavy rainfall from a severe thunderstorm that moves slowly or halts over a given area. It may also be caused by the failure of a dam or levee. (A dam is a structure that controls the rate of water flow, while a levee is a structure built to prevent water from overflowing the banks of a river.) Flash floods are the most dangerous type of floods because they develop with little warning, and it is difficult for people to escape the floodwaters.

Flash flood in Johnstown

The deadliest flash flood in the history of the United States occurred in Johnstown, Pennsylvania, on May 31, 1889. The flood was caused by the collapse of a dam, which unleashed a wall of water 36 to 40 feet (11 to 12 meters) high, in some places surging to 60 feet (18 meters) high, and weighing 20 million tons (18 million metric tons). The water rushed over four small villages and the city of Johnstown, killing 2,209 people and leaving approximately 1,000 more missing and

Words to Know

Air pressure: the pressure exerted by the weight of air over a given area of Earth's surface. Also called atmospheric pressure or barometric pressure.

Cloudburst: the heaviest type of rain, in which rain falls at a rate of 4 inches (10 centimeters) or more per hour.

Coastal flood: a flood that occurs along the coasts of a lake or ocean.

Dam: a barrier built across a river or stream that blocks and controls the flow of water.

Doppler radar: a sophisticated type of radar that relies on the Doppler effect (the change in frequency of waves emitted from a moving source) to determine wind speed and direction, as well as the direction in which precipitation is moving.

El Niño: Spanish for "the Christ child," this is an extraordinarily strong episode (occurring every two to seven years) of the annual warming of the Pacific waters off the coast of Peru and Ecuador.

Flash flood: a sudden, intense, localized flooding caused by persistent, heavy rainfall or the failure of a levee or dam.

Flood: the overflow of water onto normally dry land.

Floodplain: nearly flat land adjacent to a river that is naturally subject to periodic flooding.

presumed dead. Tens of thousands of people were left homeless, and property damage totaled $17 million.

Johnstown was founded in 1794 on the floodplain of a river valley in the Allegheny Mountains, approximately 60 miles (97 kilometers) east of Pittsburgh in southwestern Pennsylvania. (A floodplain is a nearly flat land adjacent to a river that is naturally subjected to periodic flooding.) The city is bordered by two rivers—the Little Conemaugh and the Stony Creek—which merge into the Conemaugh River at the western edge of town. The town grew as the result of the completion of the Pennsylvania Mainline Canal in 1834 and the establishment of the Pennsylvania Railroad and the Cambria Iron Company in the 1850s.

At the time of the dam break, Johnstown was a prosperous industrial town famous for the quality of its steel. The area was home to some 30,000 people. In the years preceding 1889, flooding had become increasingly common in Johnstown. At least one of the city's bordering rivers flooded once or more each year. The reason for the flooding was a combination of heavy annual rains, rapid melting of snow in the springtime, and the

Levee: a structure that raises the banks of a river; it increases the channel's water-holding capacity and makes it more difficult for water to overflow onto the surrounding land.

Pressure gradient: the rate at which air pressure decreases with horizontal distance.

Rain gauge: a vertical container that catches rain and measures the amount of rainfall.

River flood: the overflowing of the banks of a river or stream. It may be caused by excessive rain, the springtime melting of snow, blockage of water flow due to ice, or the failure of a dam or aqueduct.

River gauge: a vertical measuring stick immersed in a river to measure changes in water level.

Severe thunderstorm: a thunderstorm that produces some combination of high winds, hail, flash floods, and tornadoes.

Storm surge: a wall of water, usually from the ocean, that sweeps onto shore when the eye of a hurricane passes overhead.

Tsunami: (pronounced tsoo-NAH-mee) a wave of water generated by an underwater earthquake, landslide, or volcanic eruption.

Weather satellite: a satellite equipped with infrared and visible imaging equipment that provides views of storms and continuously monitors weather conditions around the planet.

expansion of the city outward toward the river banks. (The edges of rivers are more susceptible to floods than are areas at higher elevations.)

Faulty dam blamed for flood

The South Fork Dam, located about 14 miles (22.5 kilometers) upstream from Johnstown on the Little Conemaugh River, was the source of the flash flood on May 31, 1889. At that time, the South Fork Dam, which was 72 feet (22 meters) high and 900 feet (274 meters) wide, was said to be the largest earth dam in the country. (An earth dam is a dam constructed from layers of compacted soil.) The dam created a 2-mile-long (3.2-kilometer-long) and 1-mile-wide (1.6-kilometer-wide) reservoir called Lake Conemaugh, then the largest human-made lake in the country. Lake Conemaugh, which was 60 feet (18 meters) deep at the dam, was situated at an elevation 450 feet (137 meters) higher than Johnstown.

The dam, built in the 1840s as part of the Pennsylvania Canal System, had not had been used since 1853. In that year the railroad was completed and replaced the canals as the primary freight transport system. After that time the dam had been poorly maintained. Residents were concerned about the dam and wondered every spring if it would hold. In May 1889 their worst fears were realized.

A steady rain began falling on the afternoon of May 30, 1889, and continued all through the night and into the next day. A total of 8 inches (20 centimeters) of rain fell overnight, causing the water level at the dam to rise 2 feet (0.6 meters).

On the morning of May 31, the dam's spillway (passageway near the top of a dam through which water from the reservoir travels when the water level becomes high) was clogged with debris. Workers were sent to clear the spillway, but found the task impossible.

An engineer, John Parke, went to examine the dam. He was alarmed to see that cracks had formed in the dam and that water was leaking through. Parke, who realized that the dam was ready to collapse, sped off on his horse to warn the residents of South Fork—a small town just downstream from the dam—to evacuate to higher

Flood on the Mississippi River.

ground. He rode to the signal tower of the Pennsylvania Railroad to tell the telegraph operator to send a warning message to Johnstown, but the telegraph lines to Johnstown had been downed in the rains.

At 3:10 P.M. the dam gave way. The cascading roar of 20 million tons (18 million metric tons) of water could be heard for miles. Reverend G. W. Brown of the South Fork United Brethren Church observed the dam collapse. As reported in Kaari Ward's *Great Disasters,* "When I witnessed this, I exclaimed, 'God have mercy on the people below.' The dam melted away . . . onward dashed the flood, roaring like a mighty battle, tree-top high."

Water sweeps along debris

The floodwaters streamed through the narrow valley at speeds of 40 miles (64 kilometers) per hour en route to Johnstown. They brought death and destruction to South Fork, Mineral Point, Woodvale, and East Conemaugh—the four small villages along the way. The water swept away virtually everything it encountered, becoming a swirling mass of homes, schools, steel mills, barns, train engines, train cars, trees, bridges,

Drawing of the flood at Johnstown, Pennsylvania, 1889.

ILLUSTRATION BY W.A. ROGERS. REPRODUCED BY PERMISSION OF CORDIS-DETTMAN.

as well as living and dead people and animals. As the water descended upon the East Conemaugh yards of the Pennsylvania Railroad, one train passenger who lived to tell about it reported seeing "a seething, turbulent wall of water, whose crests seemed mountain-high, filling the entire valley and carrying everything before it as cornstalks before a gale."

People climbed on rooftops, trees, and floating debris to escape the raging swell of oily, muddy water. Many of the people thrown into the water were crushed between large objects. Adding to the danger of the floodwaters was 200,000 pounds (9,080 kilograms) of barbed wire that had been swept into the flow at the Gautier Wire Works of the Cambria Iron Company. The newly manufactured barbed wire cut and entangled anyone it contacted.

Destruction in Johnstown

The bulk of the flood's destruction occurred at the end of its path when it hit Johnstown. Because of excessive rainfall in the area, water was already flowing through the streets of the city. When clanging bells sounded a warning—just moments before the main flood reached the town—most of Johnstown's residents were already in the upper floors of their homes waiting out the deluge. Little did they know they were about to be inundated by as much water as goes over the Niagara Falls every thirty-six minutes.

Just upstream from Johnstown, raging waters engulfed the Pennsylvania Railroad's roundhouse and swept thirty train engines into the deadly flood. At 4:07 P.M. the wave, which was then 35 to 40 feet (11 to 12 meters) high, reached Johnstown. One of the first residents to view the flood was a lawyer named Horace Rose. Rose described the flood as "a great mass of timber, trees, roofs, and debris of every sort, rapidly advancing toward me, wrecking and carrying everything before it."

In the city center the flood formed a whirlpool that knocked several buildings from their foundations, including city hall and the YMCA. The waters also demolished Johnstown's newest hotel, Hulbert House, killing fifty guests.

Debris piled at stone bridge

Much of the wreckage was trapped by a huge stone railroad bridge that survived the flood. (The floodwaters were slowed by a mountain just ahead of the bridge.) Thousands of tons of material became jammed between the bridge's arches. The pile of debris was 40 feet (12 meters) high and covered more than 30 acres (12 hectares). It included parts of 1,600 homes and 280 businesses. After nightfall on May 31 the pile caught fire, burning to death eighty people who had survived the floodwaters but were trapped in the debris.

The floodwater that made it past the bridge washed into the Allegheny River at Pittsburgh. Workers there pulled debris and bodies out of the water. They also pulled to shore one notable survivor: a five-month-old baby who had traveled in the torrent for 75 miles (121 kilometers) on the floor of his wrecked home.

The list of 2,209 victims who died in the flood included 99 entire families and 396 children under ten years of age. Many of the bodies remained submerged in the river for days, and even months. Fearing an outbreak of typhus or typhoid fever (infectious diseases transmitted by contaminated water), people in cities that drew their water from the river downstream of Johnstown were warned to boil it before consumption.

Relief efforts

Within hours of the disaster, donations of goods, money, and medical assistance began arriving in Johnstown. Trains loaded with food, clothing, blankets, building materials, and coffins entered the city

The aftermath of the 1889 flood at Johnstown. REPRODUCED BY PERMISSION OF CORBIS-BETTMAN.

A Child Survivor's Account of the Flood

Among the lucky survivors of the Johnstown Flood was Gertrude Quinn Slattery, who was six years old at the time. Slattery clung to a muddy mattress as she was carried down the swollen river and was rescued by a burly working-man named Maxwell McAchren. Years later Slattery published her remembrances of May 31, 1889. The following are excerpts from Slattery's account.

> I had great faith that I would not be abandoned. While my thoughts were thus engaged, a large roof came floating toward me with about twenty people on it. I cried and called across the water to them to help me. This, of course they could not do. The roof was big, and they were all holding on for dear life, feeling every minute that they would be tossed to death. While I watched I kept praying, calling, and begging someone to save me. Then I saw a man come to the edge, the others holding him and talking excitedly. I could see they were trying to restrain him but he kept pulling to get away which he finally did, and plunged into the swirling waters and disappeared.

from Pittsburgh, New York, Philadelphia, Cincinnati, and other locations. Food was even sent from as far away as Burlingame, California, where grade schoolers collected and shipped potatoes. In all, more than $3.7 million was donated to the survivors of the Johnstown flood, from all across the United States and from eighteen foreign nations.

American Red Cross workers, including the organization's founder (and noted Civil War nurse) Clara Barton, arrived on June 5 to help survivors. They constructed shelters for people left homeless by the flood and organized the distribution of aid. The Johnstown flood was the first major relief effort of the American Red Cross since its founding in 1881.

Five years after the flood, the reconstruction of Johnstown was complete. The city eventually resumed its role as a manufacturing center.

Additional flash floods hit Johnstown

Johnstown suffered a second flash flood in 1936, in which twenty-five lives were lost. After that incident, the Army Corps of Engineers spent millions of dollars reinforcing the banks of the Little Conemaugh

Then his head appeared and I could see he was looking in my direction and I called, cried, and begged him to come to me. He kept going down and coming up, sometimes lost to my sight entirely, only to come up next time much closer to my raft. The water was now between fifteen and twenty feet deep.

As I sat watching this man struggling in the water my mind was firmly fixed on the fact that he was my saviour. At last he reached me, drew himself up and over the side of the mattress and lifted me up. I put both arms around his neck and held on to him like grim death. Together we went downstream with the ebb and flow of the reflex to the accompaniment of crunching, grinding, gurgling, splashing and crying and moaning of many. After drifting about we saw a little white building, standing at the edge of the water, apparently where the hill began. At the window were two men with poles helping to rescue people floating by. I was too far out for the poles, so the men called: 'Throw that baby over here to us.'

My hero said: 'Do you think you can catch her?'

They said: 'We can try.'

So Maxwell McAchron threw me across the water. (Some say twenty feet, others fifteen. I could never find out, so I leave it to your imagination. It was considered a great feat in the town, I know.)

and Stony Creek rivers in an attempt to prevent future flash floods. In July 1977, however, a heavy rain that washed down from the mountains overwhelmed the riverbanks around Johnstown. The ensuing flash flood claimed eighty-five lives in Johnstown and surrounding communities.

Dangerous science: How floods happen

There are two main types of floods: flash floods, which come with little warning and recede quickly; and large-scale floods, which are slow to build and slow to recede. The former type occurs on rivers or streams, in deserts, in urban areas, and in mountain canyons; the latter occur on major rivers and along coasts.

Flash floods

A flash flood is a sudden, intense, localized flood caused by persistent, heavy rainfall. Flash floods, which develop and recede much more quickly than other types of floods, are the most dangerous of all floods. In the 1970s flash floods surpassed lightning as the most

The Disaster as Reported in *The New York Times*

Beginning on June 1, 1889, *The New York Times* provided daily coverage of the Johnstown flood. The full scope of the tragedy did not become known to reporters, however, until June 3, when telegraph links were re-established with Johnstown. What follows are excerpts from *The Times* for the few days following the flood.

June 1, 1889 "Hundreds of Lives Lost"

. . . The whole tremendous volume of water swept in a resistless avalanche down the mountain side, making its own channel until it reached the South Fork of the Conemaugh, swelling it to the proportions of Niagara's rapids. . . .

Houses, factories and bridges were overwhelmed in the twinkling of an eye and with their human occupants were carried in a vast chaos down the raging torrent. . . .

One telegraph operator says he counted sixty-three bodies in twenty minutes floating past his office.

June 3, 1889 "The Desolated Valley"

Telegraphic communication with Johnstown has been re-established, and the work of succor to the living and of burial of the dead is going forward under direction of organized volunteer corps of physicians and ministers from Pittsburgh and every other city in the reach of the stricken and desolate valley. . . .

A temporary martial government has been established over the ruined city of Johnstown, under the Adjutant General of Pennsylvania, assisted by military companies from Pittsburgh and by volunteer officers. Attempts at disorder and violence by small gangs of tramps have been vigorously suppressed, and several marauders have been lynched and shot to death, for the people in the solemn earnestness of their work of succor and rescue have not the patience to wait the tedious process of law. . . .

June 7, 1889 "Peril After the Flood"

The certainty of the towns along the Conemaugh and Allegheny Valleys being subjected to ravages of an epidemic of typhus, or at least typhoid, fever this summer has been doubly assured by the course pursued by the persons who are now engaged in clearing the debris in the river at Johnstown. . . .

The flood deprived the entire district of any system of drainage, even the cesspools being destroyed. The river now flows over several hundreds of putrefying bodies, besides acting as a sewer for the entire district. The Conemaugh is a tributary of the Allegheny River, which in turn supplies most of the water used in Pittsburgh and Allegheny. In all, the number of persons the river supplies with water is nearly four hundred thousand. . . .

There has been no effort made to dig below the surface of the city as it was left by the deluge, and from the fact that, in the immediate vicinity, bodies have been found in the debris at the rate of five an hour, the logical inference is that in all likelihood there are scores of bodies mixed with the heavy timbers and other wreckage which were driven down upon the town by the flood and then covered with a thick layer of mud from the river bottom. Thus at a distance of not more than two feet below the surface there are corpses which will be a continual menace to the health of any person who remains in the vicinity. . . .

That the danger of the poisoned water is fully appreciated in Pittsburgh is evidenced this morning by the distribution of a warning by the President of the local Board of Health, instructing the citizens that henceforth they should filter and boil water needed for household purposes before it is used. The circular thus distributed says the necessity for these precautions is imperative, for already the Allegheny River water is unfit to drink.

A factory damaged by the 1889 flood in Johnstown. REPRODUCED BY PERMISSION OF THE CORBIS CORPORATION.

common weather-related cause of death in the United States. Each year flash floods kill an average of 110 people in the United States and are responsible for an average of $3 billion in property damage.

Flash floods are caused by warm-weather thunderstorms that are either slow-moving or stationary. These storms unleash huge quantities of rain over one location.

One way that a flash flood is set in motion is that the amount of rainfall exceeds the capacity of the ground to absorb it. When that happens, the rainwater runs along the surface, rather than soaking into it. It flows to the lowest point, which is generally a river, stream, or storm sewer. If the quantity of water is greater than the capacity of the drainage channel, the channel quickly overflows and a flash flood occurs. Flash flooding may also be set in motion by the failure of a dam or levee or the sudden melting of large quantities of snow and ice.

When the floodwaters surge out of their channel, they take the form of a sediment-laden wall that surges as high as 30 feet (9 meters), and in

A man selling souvenirs at the site of the Johnstown Flood.

the case of dam-breaks, even higher. The water rushes forward at speeds ranging from under 10 miles to more than 40 miles (under 16 kilometers to over 64 kilometers) per hour. These floodwaters are capable of moving objects weighing several tons, such as boulders, cars, train engines, buildings, and bridges—sometimes for several miles downstream.

Flash floods are common in mountainous areas. They occur there because the rain runs down the steep walls and becomes concentrated in canyons and valleys. For people trapped in a canyon when a flash flood begins, escape is almost impossible. One of the most destructive flash floods in recent history occurred in Colorado's Big Thompson Canyon, 50 miles (80 kilometers) west of Denver, on July 31, 1976, when 10 to 12 inches (25 to 30 centimeters) of rain—more than half the yearly average rainfall for that location—fell in just a few hours. It caused the overflow of the river running through the narrow canyon floor. A wall of water 20 feet (6 meters) high rushed forward, destroying more than 4,000 houses and killing at least 139 people. Roads were washed away, and nearly 200 vehicles were lost. Property damage totaled $35 million. About one thousand people had to be rescued by helicopter.

Urban regions are also prone to flash floods for the simple reason that rain cannot seep into concrete. Most cities have storm sewer systems that direct rainwater underground to nearby rivers. If the storm sewers become clogged or overwhelmed by the volume of water, the streets quickly become flooded.

Deserts also have hard, dry surfaces and experience flash floods. A heavy rainfall in the desert erodes the ground, creating channels called arroyos. Muddy water then rushes through the arroyos and flows in sheets along the ground. The rushing water carries sediment and rocks. A flash flood in the Mojave Desert of California once picked up a railroad locomotive and deposited it a mile away.

River floods

The primary cause of flooding in large rivers, such as the Mississippi, the Ohio, and the Missouri, is excessive, prolonged rain over a large area—sometimes hundreds of square miles (square kilometers). Large rivers also overflow due to springtime melting of snow, the blockage of water flow by ice, or the flow of waters from a series of flash floods on smaller rivers that feed into the larger river.

River floods can result when a small amount of rain falls on a blanket of snow, especially if temperatures are mild. If the ground beneath the snow is frozen, the melting snow and rain will not soak into the ground, but instead will run along the surface and drain into the river.

The likelihood of flooding is increased if chunks of ice, broken from the frozen surface of the river, block the river's flow at bridges or dams.

Coastal floods

Coastal floods occur along the coasts of oceans and large lakes. Most coastal flooding is produced by high waters associated with hurricanes. As a hurricane crosses over land, it produces a several-foot-high wall of water called a storm surge. Heavy rains produced by hurricanes as they travel over land may also result in flooding. Coastal flooding is a serious problem in countries where many people live on low-lying land near the ocean shores.

Large waves are another cause of coastal flooding. Wind waves—waves driven by the wind—are the most common type of waves. Vast storm systems that remain in one place produce large wind waves over the open water. Large wind waves, particularly when they come ashore during high tide, may cause flooding of coastal communities.

The flooded Ohio River snaking through Cincinnati, Ohio, in 1997.

El Niño and Flooding

In some parts of the world, floods are driven by El Niño (pronounced el NEE-nyo)—a current of warm water that migrates from west to east in the tropical Pacific Ocean. Every few years (known as El Niño years) the water that settles off the coast of Peru is unusually warm and remains so for an extended period of time. Typically in El Niño years, there is increased precipitation and flooding in Peru, Ecuador, Chile, Paraguay, Argentina, Uruguay, southern Brazil, southern United States, California, east-central Africa, central and eastern Europe, and western Australia.

The connection between flooding and El Niño is related to a change in air pressure across the Pacific that occurs during El Niño years. In normal (non-El Niño) conditions, air pressure is higher over the eastern Pacific, near South America, and lower over the western Pacific, near Australia. (High pressure is associated with clear skies, while low pressure is associated with cloudy skies and rain.) This pressure gradient (change in air pressure across a horizontal distance) drives the trade winds (the main surface winds in the region) from east to west, and toward the equator. The winds carry warmth and moisture, and rain-making clouds toward Australia and Indonesia.

During El Niño years, however, the air pressure in the western Pacific rises, while the air pressure in the eastern Pacific lowers. As the warm water in the eastern Pacific evaporates into the air and forms clouds, the normally dry coastal South American nations get abundant rainfall—causing flooding and erosion. At the same time, Australia, Indonesia, India, the Philippines, southern Africa, and other lands of the western Pacific experience less-than-average rainfall and sometimes drought.

Sometimes large waves take the form of tsunamis. Tsunamis (pronounced tsoo-NAH-mees) are produced by earthquakes, landslides, and volcanic eruptions on the ocean floor. Tsunamis travel as fast as 500 miles (800 kilometers) per hour and can range in size up to 100 feet (30 meters) high when they reach land.

Consequences of floods

When floods strike populated areas they destroy property, wash away roads and bridges, pollute water supplies (by washing sewage

China's Sorrow

The Yellow River of China, nicknamed "China's Sorrow," is the world's most flood-prone river. Records show that there have been about 1,500 floods on the Yellow River over the last 3,500 years, many of which killed large numbers of people. In the flood of 1887–88, between 900,000 and 2.5 million people in the crowded river valleys perished. That flood was, by far, the most devastating river flood in recorded history. The water covered some 50,000 square miles (129,500 square kilometers; an area the size of Alabama) and destroyed 300 villages. "Every night the sound of the winds and waters, and the weeping and crying, and cries for help, make a scene of unspeakable and cruel distress," wrote a journalist at the time in the *North China Herald*.

The Yellow River provides an interesting case study in the natural cycle of flooding and humans' attempts to control that flooding. The 3,000-mile-long (4,827-kilometer-long) Yellow River (the fourth-longest in the world) begins in the northern mountain province of Qinghai, high above sea level, and ends at the Yellow Sea. More than 1 billion cubic yards (76 million cubic meters) of clay and sand are carried down the river each year—enough material to encircle the planet twenty-seven times with a wall 3 feet (1 meter) high by 3 feet (1 meter) wide. Long ago, in the years before flood prevention measures, the yellowish sediment settled out of the river when the water slowed at northern China's Great Plain. This caused massive floods on the flatland surrounding the river every few years. The floods increased the fertility of the soil, making it one of the most productive

into drinking water), and threaten the lives of people. In the countryside floods destroy crops and drown livestock. In hilly or mountainous regions, floods can trigger landslides and rockslides that bury roads or houses below (see the chapter on Landslides).

Floods also have a positive consequence: they add fertility to the soil. On large rivers that are not controlled by dams or levees, floodwaters periodically (in some cases annually) spread out over the surrounding floodplain. There they deposit a layer of silt that enriches the soil. In Bangladesh, for example, excessive rainwater causes the flooding of one-fifth of the country on average each year. While this flooding has the negative effect of displacing and killing people, it performs the essential function of enriching agricultural lands. Examples of rivers regions in the world. Farmers in the area adapted their planting schedules to the cycle of flooding.

Around 2,000 years ago, however, people began building levees to control flooding on the Yellow River. And in the years since, Chinese workers have been increasing the height of those levees as well as erecting a series of dams. Today, bound by the levees, which are massive blockades on either side of the river erected to keep the water in its channel, the river level is 15 to 30 feet (4.6 to 9 meters) above the land. When an exceptionally heavy rain falls, the water sometimes breaks through or flows over the tops of the levees or bursts through the dams. (There are breaches in levees somewhere along the river two out of every three years.) The floods that occur when the pent-up water is finally released are violent and immense.

A park pavilion along the Yellow River in China.
REPRODUCED BY PERMISSION OF KEVIN R. MORRIS/CORBIS-BETTMANN.

that naturally flood and enrich the soil (although flood control measures are in place on most) include the Mississippi, the Nile (in Eastern Africa), the Huang (in Laos and Thailand), the Yangtze (in China), and the Brahmaputra (in Southern Asia).

The human factor

Human activity enters into three parts of the flood equation: the production of heavy rainfall, the likelihood that heavy rain will cause flooding, and the damage caused by floods to people and property. Specifically, global warming is believed to increase heavy rainfall; deforestation robs land of trees, the roots of which enable the soil to hold water; and the settlement of people in flood-prone areas increases the cost of floods in terms of life and property.

Global warming

Global warming is the theory that average temperatures around the world have begun to rise, and will continue to rise, due to an increase of certain gases—such as carbon dioxide—that trap heat in the atmosphere. Some scientists say that one result of global warming is an increased chance of extreme weather, such as heavy precipitation, floods, and droughts (also see the chapter on Global Warming).

Deforestation

Flooding is less likely to occur on ground with vegetation than on bare land. On heavily vegetated land much of the rain lands on leaf surfaces and eventually evaporates, never reaching the ground. The rain that does hit the ground soaks into the soil. The roots of trees and other plants create openings in the soil into which water can seep. At the same time, roots provide the soil with a structure that resists erosion.

In areas that have been deforested (all or most of the trees have been cut down) or the vegetation has been removed due to overgrazing or other reasons, rain runs over, instead of soaking into, the land. The rain washes the soil away and may cause sudden floods. In many parts of the world where deforestation is a problem, large numbers of trees are now being planted to reduce flooding.

Settlement in flood-prone regions

Floods are only a problem when they affect people and property. Many people, however, choose to live in floodplains. (In many parts of the United States, current land-use regulations prevent people from settling in floodplains.) While lands beside large rivers are rich in natural resources, provide water for industry and drinking, have fertile soil, provide a convenient means of transportation, afford recreational opportunities, and are sources of natural beauty, they are also prone to floods. People who choose to settle along ocean fronts undertake a similar risk. In the United States, about 7 percent of the country's 2.3 billion acres (929 million hectares) is prone to flooding.

Technology connection

Technological methods are used in both predicting and controlling floods. Weather forecasters use satellite images, radar images, readings taken at weather stations on the ground, and computer models to determine where and when heavy-rain-producing storms are forming. (See descriptions of these systems in the Blizzards chapter.) And hydrologists (scientists who study the distribution and properties of water on the Earth and in the atmosphere) at National Weather Service centers around the country use rain gauges (containers that catch rain and measure the amount of rainfall) and river gauges (tall measuring sticks implanted in river beds that monitor changes in water levels in rivers) to determine when and where floods are likely.

There are also many technological methods for protecting flood-plain-dwellers from floods. Those measures include building dams to control the rate of flow on rivers, levees to keep rivers from overflowing their banks, and sea walls to protect coasts from high water, as well as creating channels between rivers through which flood waters can flow. In addition, existing river channels can be dredged and made deeper to handle larger volumes of water. In some mountainous regions, water-detention basins are constructed at low altitudes to catch rain that falls on the slopes and runs downhill—before it reaches towns. The water is slowly released from the basins and flows along channels to lakes or rivers.

While all of these technological innovations reduce the effects of floods, they are not foolproof. In fact, they have the potential to actually worsen flooding. When a dam breaks or a levee fails, the forceful rushing of immense quantities of water is more destructive than natural

The construction of a runoff ditch as a flood-control measure taken to protect the city of Houston, Texas, from the overflows of the nearby Addicks River.
REPRODUCED BY PERMISSION OF CHARLES E. ROTKIN/CORBIS-BETTMANN.

flooding would have been. Flood control devices also provide inhabitants of the region with a false sense of security and encourage them to settle in areas that would be inundated if the devices should fail.

American author Mark Twain (1835–1910) summed up the losing battle to tame rivers, in particular the Mississippi River, in his book *Life on the Mississippi* as follows:

> One who knows the Mississippi will promptly aver—not aloud but to himself—that ten thousand River Commissions . . . cannot tame that lawless stream, cannot curb it or confine it, cannot say to it, 'Go here' or 'Go there,' and make it obey; cannot save a shore which it has sentenced; cannot bar its path with an obstruction which it will not tear down, dance over, and laugh at.

A flood-control structure on the Mississippi River.
REPRODUCED BY PERMISSION OF PHILIP GOULD/CORBIS-BETTMANN.

Interrupting a river's flood cycle

Dams and levees, while saving many communities from floods, also disrupt a river's natural cycle of flooding. When a river over-

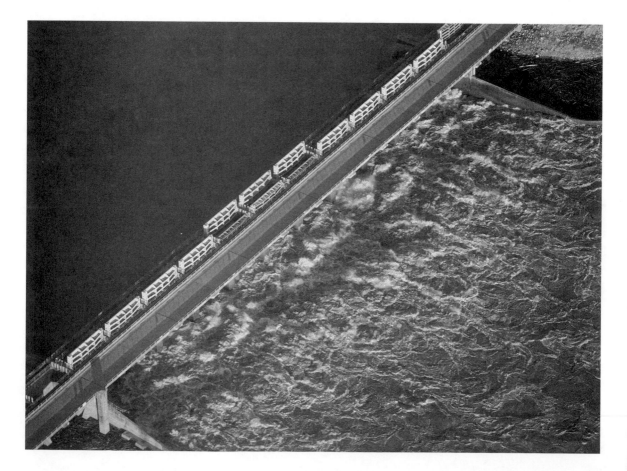

The Great Flood of 1993

"The Great Flood of 1993"—one of the largest floods in the history of the United States—occurred in the summer of 1993 along the Mississippi and Missouri rivers. Some 16,000 square miles (41,000 square kilometers) of land in Iowa, Illinois, Indiana, Minnesota, Missouri, Wisconsin, South Dakota, Nebraska, and Kansas were affected by the flood. A total of 404 counties were declared disaster areas.

Forty-eight people died in the flooding, and estimates of property damage ranged from $15 billion to $21 billion (including $6.5 billion in crop damage). Forty-five thousand homes were damaged or destroyed and 85,000 people were evacuated.

Setting the stage for the floods was a heavy snowfall throughout the Midwest the previous December. In March the snow melted, and from April through July there were record-setting rains in Minnesota, South Dakota, Iowa, Illinois, and Missouri. During a several-day period in mid-June there were daily thunderstorms in the upper Midwest. The soils in the floodplain became saturated, and reservoirs became filled to capacity.

The water reached record heights at many points along the Mississippi River, overwhelming the system of levees (built by the U.S. Army Corps of Engineers after a disastrous flood in 1927). Sixty percent of the levees failed, and the river swallowed up fifty-six towns—at some points becoming 7 miles (11 kilometers) wide.

Men rowing through a flood in Des Moines, Iowa, in 1993. REPRODUCED BY PERMISSION OF REUTERS/CORBIS-BETTMANN.

The Grand Forks Flood of 1997

In April 1997 entire towns were submerged in floodwaters when the Red River, which runs between North Dakota and Minnesota, overflowed its banks. The floods took seven lives in North Dakota and four in Minnesota. In North Dakota about 90,000 head of livestock died. Property damages throughout the Red River Valley (the areas of North Dakota and Minnesota along the banks of the Red River) totaled $3 billion. The lion's share of the destruction occurred in Grand Forks, North Dakota, 90 percent of which was put underwater.

Floods for the region had been predicted as early as February, because of the several heavy snowstorms that took place that winter. In North Dakota, houses were buried up to their roofs in snow. In March the snow began to melt and, as predicted, the rivers ran high.

The manageable spring flood was intensified by an early April storm that dumped an inch of freezing rain and sleet on the Red River Valley. Next came a blizzard with winds of 70 miles (113 kilometers) per hour. A total of 17 inches (43 centimeters) of snow and ice fell, and the air turned bitterly cold. Power lines were knocked down, as was a television tower 2,060 feet (628 meters) high (the tallest structure in the region) near Galesburg, North Dakota.

It took almost two weeks for the main impact of the snow and ice to be felt. The melting snow in southern North Dakota flowed into the Red River, causing the water level to rise there and at points downstream. (The Red River flows northward into Canada.) Ice jams blocked the flow of water near

flows into a floodplain, it deposits a layer of silt that enriches the soil. Once the river is prevented from overflowing, the fertile soil is not replenished.

When a dam is constructed, the soil upstream is buried beneath the reservoir, and the soil downstream remains exposed but becomes less fertile over time. A prime example of this phenomenon is the Nile River, on which the Aswan High Dam was constructed in 1970. The dam not only prevented the river's annual flooding, but it trapped 98 percent of the river's rich sediments. Since that time, farmers along the river have been forced to use large amounts of chemical fertilizer and are experiencing soil erosion because the river does not bring new sediments each year.

Grand Forks, and the water overflowed its banks and levees. The water quickly spread over the flat valley. Just south of Grand Forks, the Red River—typically only 100 to 200 feet (30 to 61 meters) across—reached a width of 10 miles (16 kilometers).

Grand Forks residents piled sandbags in a futile effort to protect their city from the encroaching waters. On April 18 it became clear that the floodwaters could not be stopped, and nearly all of the city's 50,000 residents were evacuated. On April 22, with the Red River 26 feet (8 meters) above flood stage, the water submerged Grand Forks and neighboring East Grand Forks, Minnesota (the residents of which had also been evacuated). The flood damaged almost every home and business in both communities.

Submerged cars in downtown East Grand Forks, Minnesota, after the nearby Red River overflowed in 1997.
REPRODUCED BY PERMISSION OF AP/WORLD WIDE PHOTOS.

A matter of survival

Flooding on large rivers, such as that produced by prolonged periods (sometimes months) of rain, can be predicted for specific locations about three days in advance. This feat is accomplished by checking water levels at various points along the river and determining the rate at which the water is rising. When a flood warning along a major river is issued, it generally means that residents in the warning area must evacuate.

Flash flood alerts are issued for localities when intense, slow-moving thunderstorms are detected. A flash flood watch means that heavy rains may cause flash flooding within the designated area. Residents are advised to prepare to evacuate to higher ground. It is also wise at that time to fill bathtubs and large containers with water for drinking and cooking in case the local water source becomes contaminated. When a flash flood warning is issued, it means that a flash flood has been reported and currently threatens the designated area. At that time, people are told to immediately move to safe ground. There may be only a few minutes before waters become dangerously high.

If you live in an area that is prone to flash floods, the following precautions are recommended:

- Learn the evacuation routes to higher ground.
- Keep your car's gas tank filled.
- Put together a supplies kit for your home containing first aid materials, a battery-powered flashlight, a battery-powered radio, extra batteries, rubber boots, rubber gloves, nonperishable food, a nonelectric can opener, and bottled water.
- Install check valves in your home's sewer traps to prevent flood water from backing up and coming in through your drains.

Encountering a flash flood

If you encounter a flash flood, the most important thing to remember is to stay out of the water. Don't try to walk, swim, or drive through it. If you're in a car, drive away from the water. If you're on foot, climb to higher ground. The water is moving rapidly and contains dangerous debris. Water traveling at just 8 miles (13 kilometers) per hour has enough force to push a car or light truck off the road. You can be knocked over by as little as 6 inches (15 centimeters) of rushing water. In addition, deeper water may have an undertow that drags you beneath the surface.

If you're driving during a heavy rainfall, keep an eye out for flooding at low spots in the road and under bridges. Those are the places that fill with water first. Be especially careful at night, when flooded areas are hard to see.

If your car stalls in moving water, get out and try to walk to higher ground. A car will float away in just 2 feet of water (just 6 inches for very small cars). The vehicle is then at the mercy of the current, which may carry it into deeper water, smash it against large objects, or overturn it. Sixty percent of people who die in flash floods are either in a car or are attempting to leave a car that has been stranded in high water.

For more information

Books

Ahrens, C. Donald. *Meteorology Today: An Introduction to Weather, Climate, and the Environment.* 5th ed. St. Paul, MN: West Publishing Company, 1994.

Armbruster, Ann. *Floods*. New York: Franklin Watts, 1996.

Burroughs, William J., Bob Crowder, et. al. *Nature Company Guides: Weather*. New York: Time-Life Books, 1996.

Clark, Champ. *Flood*. Alexandria, VA: Time-Life Books, 1982.

Cunningham, William P., et. al. *Environmental Encyclopedia*. Detroit: Gale Research, 1994.

De Blij, Harm J., et al. *Restless Earth*. Washington, DC: National Geographic Society, 1997, pp. 20–21.

Engelbert, Phillis. *Complete Weather Resource*. Farmington Hills, MI: U•X•L, 1997.

Forces of Nature. Alexandria, VA: Time-Life Books, 1990.

Hawkes, Nigel. *New Technology: Structures and Buildings*. New York: Twenty-First Century Books, 1994, pp. 26–27.

Keller, Ellen. *Floods!* New York: Simon Spotlight, 1999.

Knapp, Brian. *Flood*. Austin, TX: Steck-Vaughn, 1990.

Nature on the Rampage. With Harm J. De Blij. Washington, DC: Smithsonian Books, 1994.

Patton, Peter C. "Floods," in *Encyclopedia of Earth Sciences*. E. Julius Dasch, ed. New York: Macmillan Library Reference, 1996, pp. 314–317.

Powers of Nature. Washington, DC: National Geographic Society, 1978.

Robinson, Andrew. *Earth Shock: Hurricanes, Volcanoes, Earthquakes, Tornadoes and Other Forces of Nature*. New York: Thames and Hudson, 1993.

Rosenfeld, Jeffrey. *Eye of the Storm: Inside the World's Deadliest Hurricanes, Tornadoes, and Blizzards*. New York: Plenum Trade, 1999.

Rozens, Aleksandrs. *Floods*. New York: Twenty-First Century Books, 1994.

Ward, Kaari, ed. *Great Disasters*. Pleasantville, NY: Reader's Digest Association, 1989, pp. 146–149.

Waterlow, Julia. *Flood*. New York: Thomson Learning, 1992.

Williams, Jack. *The Weather Book: An Easy-to-Understand Guide to the USA's Weather*. New York: USA Today & Vintage Books, 1992.

Wright, Russell G. *Flood!* Menlo Park, CA: Addison-Wesley Publishing Company, 1996.

Zebrowski, Ernest Jr. *Perils of a Restless Planet: Scientific Perspectives on Natural Disasters*. New York: Cambridge University Press, 1997.

Periodicals

Cobb, Kathy. "North Dakota, Minnesota: The Forks Continue Flood Recovery Plans." *Fedgazette (Minneapolis)*. (July 1998): p. 12+.

"Deforestation Blamed in Part for Mexico Flooding." Associated Press. (September 21, 1998).

Flood

Henson, Robert. "Up to Our Necks: In 1997, the Floods Just Wouldn't Stop." *Weatherwise*. (March/April 1998): pp. 22–25.

Le Comte, Douglas. "The Weather of 1997: The Year of the Floods." *Weatherwise*. (March/April 1999): pp. 14–21.

———. "The Weather of 1998: A Warm, Wet, and Stormy Year." *Weatherwise*. (March/April 1999): pp. 19–21.

"New Controls Tamed in Nevada Floods, Experts Say." *The New York Times*. (July 10, 1999): p. A9.

U.S. Dept. of Commerce. *Flash Floods and Floods—The Awesome Power!* Washington, DC: NOAA, 1992.

Web sites

"Dealing with the Deluge." *NOVA Online* [Online] http://www.pbs.org/wgbh/nova/flood/deluge.html (accessed on March 8, 2001).

Johnstown Flood Museum. [Online] http://www.jaha.org (accessed on March 8, 2001).

"Johnstown Flood by The New York Times." *Johnstown Pennsylvania Information Source Online.* [Online] http://www.johnstownpa.com/History/hist30.html (accessed on March 8, 2001).

"A Roar Like Thunder . . ." *Johnstown Pennsylvania Information Source Online.* [Online] http://www.johnstownpa.com/History/hist19.html (accessed on March 8, 2001).

"USA Today Weather." *USA Today.* [Online] http://www.usatoday.com/weather/ (accessed on March 8, 2001).

Videocassettes

Raging Planet: Flood. Directed by Mick Rhodes. Discovery Channel, 1998. (Distributed by BMG Entertainment, New York.)

global warming

8

Global warming is the theory that average temperatures around the world have begun to rise, and will continue to rise, because of an increase of certain gases in Earth's atmosphere. These gases are called "greenhouse gases" because they trap heat just like a greenhouse. They let sunlight come in, but don't let heat go back out into space. The most plentiful greenhouse gases are water vapor and carbon dioxide; others include methane, nitrous oxide, and chlorofluorocarbons.

The increase of carbon dioxide in the atmosphere is believed to be the main reason for global warming. Carbon dioxide is produced by burning fossil fuels—such as coal, fuel oil, gasoline, and natural gas— and is emitted into the air from homes, factories, and motor vehicles. During the last century, the amount of carbon dioxide in the atmosphere has increased 30 percent. During that same period, the planet has become, on average, slightly more than 1°F (0.5°C) warmer.

Since 1880, when accurate temperatures were first recorded around the world, 1998 was the world's warmest year, and 1995, 1996, 1997, and 1999 were among the ten warmest years on record. In fact, tree rings and sea coral growth indicate that the 1990s was the hottest decade in the last 1,000 years. (Trees and sea corals grow outward from the center, depositing concentric rings every year; each ring yields information about rainfall and temperature for that year.)

David Rind, a researcher with National Aeronautics and Space Administration's Goddard Institute for Space Studies, commented in the November 6, 2000, issue of *U.S. News & World Report* that warming in the twentieth century was "a magnitude of change that hasn't been seen for thousands of years." According to an October 2000 United Nations report, if present trends continue we can expect an average

Words to Know

Deforestation: the removal of all or most of the trees from an area.

Drought: (pronounced DROWT) an extended period during which the amount of rain or snow that falls on an area is much lower than usual.

Ecosystem: a community of plants and animals, including humans, and their physical surroundings.

El Niño: (pronounced el NEE-nyo) means "the Christ child" in Spanish. A period of unusual warming of the Pacific Ocean waters off the coast of Peru and Ecuador. It usually starts around Christmas, which is how it got its name.

Electric vehicles: vehicles that run on electric batteries and motors instead of gasoline-powered engines.

Food chain: the transfer of food energy from one organism to another. It begins with a plant species, which is eaten by an animal species; it continues with a second animal species, which eats the first, and so on.

Fossil fuels: coal, oil, and natural gas—materials composed of the remains of plants or animals that covered Earth millions of years ago and are today burned for fuel.

global temperature increase of 2.7 to 11°F (1.5 to 6.2°C) by the year 2100. That amount of warming is capable of melting substantial amounts of polar ice, raising sea levels by several feet, and increasing the severity of storms. To understand the magnitude of this change, it is helpful to note that during the last ice age global temperatures were only an average of 5 to 9°F (2.8 to 5°C) lower than they are today. Scientists studying global warming using sophisticated computer programs predict that Earth's climate will undergo as great a change in the next century as it has in the last 10,000 years.

Global warming is dangerous because it has the potential to disrupt ecosystems and bring about the extinction of numerous species of plants and animals. Many scientists blame global warming for the increasing number of severe storms, as well as droughts and floods, around the planet. Rising sea levels—another consequence of global warming—threatens to put island nations and coastal cities underwater.

Rising sea levels

Because of global warming, ocean levels have increased 4 to 10 inches (10 to 25 centimeters) since 1900. The rate at which the sea level

Global warming: the theory that the average temperatures around the world have begun to rise, and will continue to rise, because of an increase of certain gases (called greenhouse gases) in Earth's atmosphere.

Greenhouse effect: the warming of Earth due to the presence of greenhouse gases, which trap upward-radiating heat and return it to Earth's surface.

Greenhouse gases: gases that trap heat in the atmosphere. The most abundant greenhouse gases are water vapor and carbon dioxide. Others include methane, nitrous oxide, and chlorofluorocarbons.

Heat wave: an extended period of high heat and humidity.

Hybrid vehicles: vehicles that run on more than one source of power, such as gasoline and electricity.

La Niña: (pronounced el NEE-nya) a period of unusual cooling of the Pacific Ocean waters off the coast of Peru and Ecuador. It often follows an El Niño.

Solar power: power, usually in the form of electricity or heat, derived from the Sun's radiation.

Wind power: power, usually in the form of electricity, derived from the wind.

is rising is expected to increase in the coming century. Current projections have ocean levels climbing as much as 2.5 feet (0.8 meter) by the year 2100. Such an increase would put many coastal areas underwater.

The primary reason for rising water levels is that ocean water becomes less dense and expands as its temperature increases. Water from melting glaciers in Greenland, Alaska, and Antarctica, as well as in the Rockies, Urals, Alps, Andes, also contributes to rising sea levels.

"The melting of glaciers is emerging as one of the least ambiguous signs of climate change," wrote science writer Fred Pearce in the March 31, 2000, *Independent* of London. "Amid arcane arguments about the meaning of yearly fluctuations in the weather, it is hard to argue with the wholesale melting of some of the largest glaciers in the world. Mankind, it seems, has hit the defrost button."

Melting in Antarctica

The melting of the West Antarctic ice sheet—an enormous glacier in Antarctica—poses the greatest threat to coastal cities and island nations. At its thickest point, the ice sheet is 9.75 miles (15.7 kilometers) deep—ten times the height of the tallest skyscraper in the United States.

And because the ice sheet sits on land below sea level, ocean waters lap at its edges and make it vulnerable to melting.

If the West Antarctic ice sheet were to collapse and pour into the sea, it would raise global sea levels by 13 to 20 feet (4 to 6 meters). A sea-level rise of that size would flood coastal regions, including much of Florida and New York City. Global warming experts, however, believe that it would take 500 to 700 years for the West Antarctic ice sheet to collapse if global warming continues at its present rate.

Melting in Greenland

The melting of Greenland's ice sheet—the world's second largest expanse of ice after all of Antarctica's ice—is also a grave concern. The Greenland ice is 2 miles (3.2 kilometers) thick on average and covers 708,000 square miles (1.84 million square kilometers)—almost all of Greenland.

Studies conducted by the National Aeronautic and Space Administration (NASA) between 1993 and 1999 show that Greenland's ice is thinning on about 70 percent of its margins—in some places by 3 feet (1 meter) per year. In total, more than 2 cubic miles (8.2 cubic kilometers) of Greenland's ice melts each year. That amount of melting accounts for about 7 percent of the yearly rise in sea levels. If Greenland's entire ice sheet were to melt, ocean levels would rise by several feet, and there would be massive flooding in many parts of the world.

Heat waves emanating from Earth in this computer-enhanced image of the effect of global warming.
REPRODUCED BY PERMISSION OF PICTURE PRESS/CORBIS-BETTMANN.

Melting in the Himalayas

The Himalayan Mountains, one-sixth of which are covered with glaciers, contain more snow and ice than any other place in the world except for the polar regions. (The Himalayas cover 1,500 miles [2,340 kilometers] across northern India, Nepal, and Tibet.) In the summer of 1999, researchers from Jawaharlal Nehru University in Delhi, India, announced their findings that the Himalayan glaciers are melting faster than glaciers anywhere else in the world. Their study showed that the Gangotri glacier, situated at the head of the Ganges River—a 1,550-mile-long (2,418-kilometers-long) river flowing southeast from the Himalayas into the Bay of Bengal—is shrinking at a rate of approximately 90 feet (27 meters) per year. If melting in the Himalayas continues at present levels, those glaciers could disappear by the year 2035.

The meltwaters from the Himalayan glaciers have formed dozens of lakes, many of which arc in danger of bursting. The water in these lakes is held back by natural dams—walls of debris that were deposited by

Aerial view of ice cap in Greenland breaking into the sea. REPRODUCED BY PERMISSION OF JAMES L. AMOS/CORBIS-BETTMANN.

retreating glaciers over the last 300 years. As the water level in these lakes continues to rise, it puts pressure on the natural dams. Eventually, the force of the water could grow too great, and the dam could give way, causing a wall of water to surge down the mountainside. Such catastrophes used to occur about once every ten years, but for the last decade, however, they have been occurring once every three years. Geologists anticipate that by 2010, lake-bursts in the Himalayas will be annual events.

The worst lake-burst in recent history took place in 1985 in the Khumbal Himal region of Nepal. A wall of water 50 feet (15 meters) high swept downstream, killing villagers and destroying a hydroelectric plant. In 1994 a lake-burst in northern Bhutan killed twenty-seven people and ruined buildings and farmland. In the summer of 2000, engineers were hard at work shoring up a lake at the edge of the Trakarding glacier, northeast of Katmandu. If that lake, which sits above a populated area, were to collapse, it could drown some 7,000 people. As of the fall of 2000, scientists had identified seven lakes in imminent danger of collapse. A glacial lake in Nepal's Sagarmatha Park, for instance, is expected to burst by the year 2004.

The increased melting of the Himalayan glaciers also threatens to disrupt the region's supply of water for drinking and crop irrigation. Glacial meltwaters supply two-thirds of the flow of the Ganges River and other nearby waterways. If the glaciers melt entirely, those rivers will shrink and cease to supply the region. If that happens, almost 500 million people in India would be at risk of starvation.

Island nations in trouble

The effects of the swollen seas are already being felt by small island nations. On the South Pacific islands of Kiribati and Tuvalu, for example, rising waters have destroyed roads and bridges and washed out traditional burial grounds. Many residents of those islands have had to move to higher ground. And in Barbados, rising ocean levels have caused salt water to contaminate fresh-water wells near the coasts. The salination (process of making salty) of drinking water is a grave concern in Barbados, where drinking water is already in short supply.

At the global warming summit held in The Hague in November 2000 (see section "The Human Factor" on page 211), representatives of thirty-nine small island nations expressed their frustration at rising sea levels. They described the threat that rising waters pose to tourism and agriculture, which are concentrated on the coasts and are primary sources of income for island nations. "These are serious issues of economics and livelihood—issues that can disrupt the social fabric of countries," stated Leonard Nurse, a representative from Barbados in a news report of November 17, 2000.

Nurse and other delegates from island nations responded angrily to suggestions made that they should cope with rising sea levels by building surge barriers and storm drains. They blamed industrialized nations, foremost among them the United States, for placing large amounts of carbon dioxide in the air and accelerating global warming. Those sentiments were underscored by Yumie Crisostomo of the Marshall Islands, who stated to the press: "Whoever caused the problem has to clear up the problem."

Dangerous science: What causes global warming?

Global warming is the result of an increase in Earth's natural greenhouse effect—the process by which Earth's atmosphere is warmed. While the term "greenhouse effect" has a negative popular connotation because of its association with pollution and global warming, it also has its positives. If the greenhouse effect didn't exist, our planet's surface would not be warm enough to sustain life. In fact, without the greenhouse effect, Earth's average surface temperature would be the same as its outer atmosphere, about 0°F (–18°C).

How the greenhouse effect works

The greenhouse effect is so-named because of the similarity of the heat-trapping function of Earth's atmosphere to that of a greenhouse.

Snow-covered Himalayan peak, India. REPRODUCED BY PERMISSION OF RIC ERGENBRIGHT/CORBIS-BETTMANN.

The glass panels of a greenhouse allow solar radiation to pass through. The plants and other objects in the greenhouse absorb the radiation, converting it to heat. Some of that heat is then re-radiated upward, where it is absorbed by the glass. The glass then re-radiates some of that heat downward, back to the plants.

"Greenhouse gases" (i.e., water vapor, carbon dioxide, methane, nitrous oxide, and chlorofluorocarbons) act like the glass of a greenhouse in that they trap heat. Specifically, greenhouse gases trap heat in Earth's atmosphere. The process begins as solar radiation enters the atmosphere in the form of visible light. Earth's surface absorbs that radiation and converts it to infrared radiation (heat), which has a shorter wavelength than light. Some of the heat rises and is absorbed by greenhouse gases in the atmosphere. The gases re-radiate heat outward in all directions, including back toward the surface. By this process Earth's lower atmosphere is heated continuously, even at night when there is no incoming solar radiation.

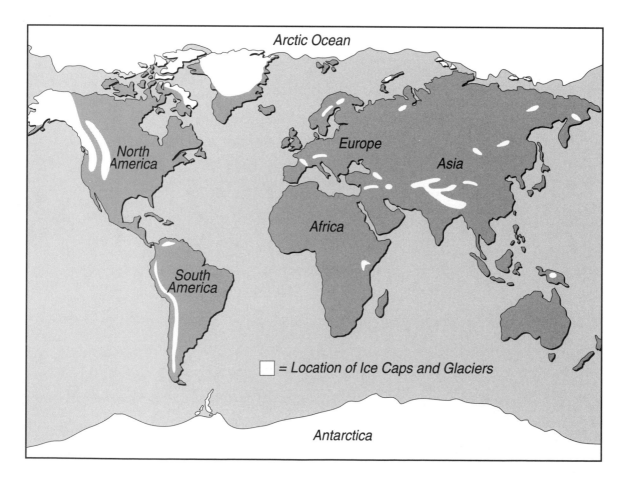

Why Melting Icebergs Don't Contribute to Rising Sea Levels

Many people are under the false impression that melting icebergs—as well as the melting of the floating ice cap that covers the waters around the North Pole—are contributing to the rise in sea level. In fact, the melting of floating ice has the opposite effect—it actually lowers the sea level. Ice, with its crystalline configuration of molecules, takes up more space than liquid water. The following experiment demonstrates this principle:

1. Take a large clear bowl and fill it halfway with water.

2. Empty a tray of ice cubes into the water and measure the height of the water.

3. Wait for the ice to melt, and then measure the height of the water again. You will notice that the water level has decreased.

The most plentiful, and most effective, greenhouse gas is water vapor. And the greatest concentration of water vapor is found within clouds. For this reason, all other things being equal, the surface temperature remains higher on cloudy nights than it does on clear nights. During the day, however, clouds have the opposite effect. Since clouds block incoming solar radiation, they have a cooling effect on the surface during the day.

You may now be wondering why the greenhouse effect has been getting so much negative publicity in recent years, when it is necessary to sustain life. The answer is that too much of a good thing, in this case the warming of Earth, can be harmful. The natural systems on Earth exist in a delicate balance and require a specific temperature range. If the heat is turned up, the balance is disrupted. The concentration of some greenhouse gases has increased rapidly in recent years, meaning that more heat is being trapped and returned to Earth. This condition is technically called enhanced greenhouse effect, but is better known as global warming.

Carbon dioxide is the main culprit

An increase in the amount of carbon dioxide in the atmosphere is the primary reason for the enhanced greenhouse effect. Carbon dioxide is an industrial by-product that has been accumulating in the atmosphere since the Industrial Revolution (1760–1830). Carbon dioxide is produced by the burning of coal, oil, gas, and wood and is emitted by factory smokestacks and motor vehicles.

Levels of carbon dioxide, measured at the Mauna Loa Observatory in Hawaii, rose from about 315 parts per million (ppm) in 1960 to about 350 ppm in 1990. During the last century the level of carbon dioxide in the air has risen by 25 percent. As of 2001, the rate of increase of carbon dioxide in the atmosphere was about 0.5 percent per year.

Another reason why levels of carbon dioxide are increasing is deforestation—the clearing of the forests. Deforestation affects the atmosphere in two ways. First, trees naturally absorb carbon dioxide by converting it to oxygen through the process of photosynthesis. With fewer trees, less carbon dioxide is absorbed. Second, in clearing forests to allow for other land use (such as farming), many trees are burned; this places large amounts of carbon dioxide into the atmosphere.

Other greenhouse gases

Carbon dioxide is not the only pollutant responsible for enhancing the greenhouse effect. Concentrations of other greenhouse gases, such as chlorofluorocarbons (CFCs), nitrous oxides, and methane, are also on the rise. While the concentrations of each of these other gases is substantially smaller than the concentration of carbon dioxide, these gases are much more efficient than carbon dioxide at absorbing infrared radiation.

An atmosphere with natural levels of greenhouse gases (left) compared to an atmosphere of increased greenhouse effect (right).

CFCs are human-made hydrocarbons, such as freon, in which some or all of the hydrogen atoms have been replaced by fluorine atoms. CFCs can be liquids or gases and are used in refrigerators and air conditioners; as propellants in aerosol spray cans (such as deodorants, spray paints, and hairsprays) and foam-blowing canisters; and in some cleaning solvents.

Nitrous oxides, like carbon dioxide, are emitted from industrial smokestacks and car exhaust systems. They are also components of some fertilizers sprayed on agricultural fields.

Methane is a product of anaerobic (in the absence of oxygen) decay of organic matter. Some sources of methane are swamps, the digestive systems of cattle, rice paddies, and garbage dumps. By raising livestock, growing rice for millions of people, and dumping refuse in landfills, humans are contributing to a rising concentration of methane in the atmosphere.

Consequences of global warming

Current predictions about the trend in global warming maintain that within the next century the world may reach its warmest point in the history of civilization. The effects, according to many scientists, could be disastrous. One consequence of global warming, as discussed above, is an increase in ocean levels around the world. The warmer weather is also expected to alter rainfall patterns, increase the severity

The Mauna Loa Weather Observatory in Hawaii. REPRODUCED BY PERMISSION OF JAMES L. AMOS/CORBIS-BETTMANN.

of storms, and have negative effects on human health. And by many accounts, global warming has already harmed certain animal species.

Drought, floods, and storms

Global warming is expected to increase the amount of rainfall in the tropics and produce drought (pronounced DROWT) throughout temperate regions (for example, the northern three-quarters of the United States, southern Canada, and much of Europe). In places suffering from a lack of rainfall, crop yields would be lower, and natural vegetation would suffer. Grazing animals would either have to migrate to find food and water or would die off.

Climatologists (scientists who study climate) point to the occurrence, over the last two decades, of two of the strongest El Niños on record as further evidence of global warming. (El Niño is the extraordinarily strong episode of the annual warming of the Pacific waters off the coast of Peru; for more information see the chapter on El Niño.)

Some scientists also assert that global warming has been responsible for recent, unusually severe weather, such as strong blizzards, hurricanes, tornadoes, heat waves, and wildfires. They warn that these weather disasters will intensify as global warming increases. Other scientists dispute the effect of global warming on the weather, pointing out that there has been no increase in the number of major hurricanes in recent decades.

Dangers to human health

By many accounts, global warming is bad for human health. The United Nations' Intergovernmental Panel on Climate Change (IPCC), a group consisting of 2,500 of the world's leading climatologists, in its year 2000 report, concluded that global warming may cause a "significant loss of [human] life." The warmer weather has been linked to worsening air pollution, more severe heat waves, and increased populations of disease-carrying insects and rodents. The IPCC predicts that 60 percent of the world population will be vulnerable to malaria (a disease spread by mosquitoes) by the year 2100 (up from 45 percent in 2000). And a group of researchers in the United States warns that the number of U.S. residents dying of heat stress may double by the year 2075. (Presently 2,000 to 3,000 people per year die from heat stress.)

Sustained rains, predicted for warm regions, may produce flooding that causes drinking water to be contaminated with sewage; people drinking the contaminated water would become sick. Warmer air also increases ground-level ozone pollution (smog), which aggravates symptoms of asthma and other respiratory ailments.

The warmer air allows some diseases to move farther north, affecting new populations. "It's happening right now," stated Paul Epstein, associate director of the Center for Health and Global Environment at Harvard University's Medical School, in an August 2000 newspaper report. "Glaciers are retreating, plants are migrating. We're seeing West Nile virus in New York, dengue and malaria in northern India."

Disruptions to animal life

Many scientists are also concerned about the harm global warming causes to wildlife. "Global climate change has the potential to wipe out more species, faster, than any other single factor," stated Patty Glick, coordinator of the Climate Change and Wildlife Program at the National Wildlife Federation, in a November/December 2000 *International Wildlife* interview. The World Wildlife Fund estimates that 20

A farmer in the Netherlands surveys his land as the chimneys of a power station fill the atmosphere with pollution. REPRODUCED BY PERMISSION OF ADAM WOOLFIT/CORBIS-BETTMANN.

percent of species in northern regions, from New England to the North Pole, could die out by the year 2100 because of the loss of habitat brought about by global warming.

As reported by the World Wildlife Federation in June 1999, tropical fish have been forced to migrate to colder waters in search of food. Animals that depend on fish for sustenance (such as sharks, sea lions, and marine birds) have also been forced to migrate or face starvation.

The reason for the migration is that the warming of ocean waters in recent years has led to a reduction of the fishes' food source, ocean plankton, in waters where plankton have traditionally thrived. Plankton are microscopic plants (phytoplankton) and animals (zooplankton) that occupy the bottom rung of the food chain. Off the west coast of North America, plankton populations have decreased by 70 percent since 1977. As a result of that change, there has been a 90 percent decline in seabird populations since 1987.

Arctic animals in trouble

The effects of global warming on wildlife are seen most vividly in the arctic. In parts of that far northern region, temperatures have increased 7 to 10°F (4 to 5.6°C) in the thirty-five year span from 1965 to 2000. During the 1990s the number of salmon in Alaska's rivers decreased dramatically, as did the numbers of Stellar sea lions and harbor seals in the Bering Sea and Gulf of Alaska. More than 1 million seabirds starved to death in the Bering Sea in the years 1997 and 1998 alone, because of dwindling food supplies in the warmer waters.

The warmer weather also triggered much heavier snowfalls in Alaska. For some animals, such as the Peary caribou, the large quantities of snow make it difficult to get to buried food. This factor has led to a reduction in the numbers of this species of small caribou from 24,500 in 1961 to only about 1,000 in the year 2000.

Antarctic penguin species declining

Another animal species suffering from higher temperatures in recent years is the Adelie penguin. The Adelies live on the Antarctic continent and on the great sheets of off-shore pack ice. They survive on krill, tiny shrimplike animals that live in the icy waters. The krill, in turn, feed on the algae that bloom within the layers of sea ice and are released into the water as the ice melts.

The Adelies' reproductive cycle is tied to the changing of the seasons. They give birth just at the start of the Antarctic summer, when algae fill the water and krill are plentiful. If the temperature is too high and the thawing begins too early, however, the algae are scattered far and wide (as are the krill) at the time the chicks are born. In that case, the Adelie parents are forced to travel great distances to gather food for their young, all the while leaving their young unattended. A study found that Adelies were spending sixteen hours a day to gather food, up drastically from previous years' average of six hours a day. As a consequence, the young may not get enough food or may fall prey to predatory birds called skuas.

Over the last twenty-five years, Adelie penguin populations in areas under study by American researchers have declined dramatically. Numbers of breeding pairs in five large colonies dropped from 15,200 to 9,200, and several small colonies were entirely wiped out. In the last two years alone, the Adelie population in the study area dropped by 10 percent. The decline in Adelies corresponds to an increase in temperature over the last fifty years, during which time Antarctica has become warmer by 3 to 5°F (1.7 to 2.8°C) in the summer and 10°F (5.6°C) in the winter. Seals, whales, and other species of penguins are also threatened by dwindling krill supplies near Antarctica. For example, an average blue whale eats 4 to 6 tons (3.6 to 5.4 metric tons) of krill each day

The human factor

Since global warming was identified as a problem in the 1970s, there has been vigorous debate over what role, if any, human activity plays in the trend. Since 1995, however, a majority of global climate sci-

Adelie penguin on the Antarctic Peninsula. REPRODUCED BY PERMISSION OF WOLFGANG KAEHLER/CORBIS-BETTMANN.

Things Don't Look Good for the United States

In June 2000, a report commissioned by the U.S. Congress painted a grim picture of the effect of global warming on the United States. The national assessment report, compiled by scientists from both within and outside of the government, gave a detailed summary of what will likely occur if average temperatures rise 5 to 10°F (2.8 to 5.6°C) over the next century. While recognizing the "significant uncertainties in the science underlying climate-change impacts," the study concluded that "based on the best available information, most Americans will experience significant impacts" from global warming.

The report predicted that as temperatures rise, entire ecosystems will move northward. For instance, as New England warms, that region's sugar maple forests will be pushed into Canada. Salmon currently inhabiting the Columbia River (in the Pacific Northwest) will migrate northward, leaving the Columbia to warmer-water fish species. The report also warned that rising sea levels may cause coastal marshes and wetlands to spread inland, completely submerging the barrier islands off the coast of the Carolinas.

Among the report's other projections were sweltering heat waves in urban areas, frequent droughts in the Midwest, the conversion of forests in the Southeast into grasslands, the reduction of water levels in the Great Lakes (because of increased evaporation), and damage to roads and buildings in Alaska due to the thawing of the ground.

entists agree that pollution is causing global warming and that immediate action is necessary. The Intergovernmental Panel on Climate Change (IPCC) wrote the following in 1995: "The balance of evidence suggests a discernible human influence on global climate." Between the years 1995 and 2000, according to an end-of-century report by the National Research Council, global warming accelerated by 30 percent.

In the year 1999, the evidence supporting human influence on global warming became even stronger. By all accounts that year, which was a La Niña year, should have been relatively cool—but instead it was the second warmest year on record in the United States and the fifth warmest in the world. (La Niña is a period of unusual cooling of the Pacific Ocean waters off the coast of Peru and Ecuador. It generally drives global temperatures downward. In 1999, water temperatures were their lowest since 1994.) The most obvious explanation for the 1999's warmth is that emission of greenhouse gases more than offset La Niña's cooling, therefore driving temperatures even higher. "When you have a very warm year that occurs during a La Niña," commented NASA senior climate scientist Roy W. Spencer in a January 13, 2000 newspaper article, "that makes it more difficult to argue against the reality of global warming."

The IPCC placed blame for global warming on humans in its year 2000 report as follows: "It is likely that [greenhouse gases from human activities] have contributed substantially to the observed warming over the last 50 years." And Robert Watson, a climatologist and chair of the IPCC, was emphatic in stressing the human factor in the global warming equation. In a December 4, 2000 *Newsweek* article Watson stated, "There is absolutely no question that the climate is warming, sea levels are rising, and glaciers are melting. There is no question humans are involved."

Scientists from a variety of public and private agencies recommend that governments regulate greenhouse gas emissions now, instead of waiting until the problem is worse and the remedy more costly. They warn that even if the emission of pollutants were curbed

The polluted skyline of Mexico City.
REPRODUCED BY PERMISSION OF
ARCHIVE PHOTOS, INC.

today, it would take many years for the global warming trend to stop (primarily because heat, stored in the oceans, would continue to be slowly released).

Some say global warming is a natural phenomenon

Some scientists and industrialists remain skeptical that humans are turning up the heat. They point out that annual average temperatures in the continental United States have varied from decade to decade, with no significant upward or downward trend throughout the century. It was relatively cool from the beginning of the century until 1920; warmed up in the 1920s through the 1950s; cooled down in the 1960s and 1970s; and began warming again in the 1980s. One theory suggested to explain the warm 1990s is that the heat given off by the sun has increased.

Throughout Earth's 4.6 billion-year-history, the climate has undergone continuous change. There have been alternating periods of relative coolness and warmth. There have been ice ages, during which significant portions of Earth have been covered with ice and periods when the world was warmer than it is now. And there is every reason to believe that climate change is naturally occurring today, as it will in the future.

Humans have only been on Earth for 2 million years—less than 0.05 percent of our planet's lifetime. The earliest records of human civilization are only about 6,000 years old. And accurate weather records began just a century ago in many parts of the world. All of these factors raise the question: given our relatively brief existence on the planet, is it possible that human activities are responsible for creating long-term climate change?

Some scientists and business leaders make the argument that humans have little, if any, role in global warming. They claim that human activity is insignificant compared to all the natural factors that interact to bring about global climate change. They caution that misguided fossil fuel-reduction policies could harm the economy.

S. Fred Singer, atmospheric physicist at Washington University in St. Louis, Missouri, and author of the 2000 report "What Do We Know About Human Influence on Climate Change?" argues that global warming will likely be insignificant and may even have beneficial effects. Singer asserts that a slight global warming will increase growing seasons and be good for agriculture, and that efforts to slow global warming would be costly and ineffective.

In recent years, however, a growing number of corporations have abandoned the position that global warming is not a social problem. Among the companies now recognizing the possibility of humans' contribution to global warming and endorsing pollution controls are oil giant British Petroleum-Amoco, the American Electric Power Company, Shell Oil, Dow Chemical, and Ford Motor Company.

Earth Summit addresses global warming

The debate over the role of human activity in global warming has been carried out all over the world. The first international meeting to address the problem of global warming was held in June 1992 in Rio de Janeiro, Brazil. Formally called the U.N. Conference on Environment and Development, but better known as the Earth Summit, the 1992 meeting was attended by representatives of 178 nations—including 117 heads of state.

A rushing stream is formed from the meltwater of the Franz Josef Glacier in New Zealand.

REPRODUCED BY PERMISSION OF RICHARD HAMILTON SMITH/CORBIS-BETTMANN.

One outcome of the Earth Summit was the drafting of a document called the Declaration on Environment and Development, also known as the Rio Declaration. The document spelled out twenty-seven guiding principles of environmentally friendly economic development. Conference attendees came to an informal agreement on the need to change energy policies in order to halt global warming. The Rio Declaration begins as follows:

1. Human beings are at the center of concerns for sustainable development. They are entitled to a healthy and productive life in harmony with nature.

2. States have the right to exploit their own resources pursuant to their own environmental and developmental policies, and the responsibility to ensure that activities within their jurisdiction do not cause damage to the environment of other nations.

3. The right to development must be fulfilled so as to equitably meet developmental and environmental needs of present and future generations.

4. In order to achieve sustainable development, environmental protection shall constitute an integral part of the development process.

Global warming talks continue at Kyoto convention

In December 1997 representatives of 166 nations gathered in Kyoto, Japan, for the United Nations (U.N.) Framework Convention on Climate Change. The conference focused on the growing problem of global warming and ways to reduce greenhouse emissions.

Delegates to the meeting produced the Kyoto protocol—a document that called upon industrialized nations (relatively wealthy nations, such as those in North America and western Europe) to take the lead in reducing emissions of greenhouse gases. The protocol specifically called on thirty-six industrialized nations to reduce greenhouse-gas emissions between the years 2008 and 2012 to 5.2 percent below 1990 levels. Poorer developing nations (in Africa, Latin America, parts of Asia, and the Middle East) were spared the treaty's requirements. Conference participants agreed that it would pose too great an economic burden on developing nations to greatly reduce greenhouse emissions.

Another reason why the burden was placed on industrialized nations is that those nations are the largest producers of greenhouse gases. The United States, for instance, is responsible for 25 percent of global carbon dioxide emissions—that's more than any other nation. In 1995 the United States emitted 5.8 billion tons (5.2 billion metric tons) of carbon dioxide. Russia placed second with 2 billion tons (1.8 billion metric tons), and Japan placed third with 1.2 billion tons (1.1 billion metric tons). The United States' carbon dioxide emissions are expected to grow by 30 percent between 1998 and 2008.

"We must . . . approach a sustainable energy use and find a solution to the threat of global warming early in the twenty-first century," stated Gro Harlem Bruntland, chairperson of the U.N. World Commission on Environment and Development and an organizer of the conference, in a published report. "Such a commitment would require a degree of shared vision and common responsibilities new to humanity. Success lies in the force of imaginations. . . . "

United States fails to ratify Kyoto accord. In November 1998 the Clinton administration endorsed the Kyoto protocol. That signing of the document, however, was largely symbolic since the Senate did not give its approval. (The U.S. Constitution states that all treaties are subject to ratification by two-thirds of the Senate.) Given the treaty's certain defeat in the Senate, President Clinton chose not to put it to a vote.

Senate leaders made their concerns about the Kyoto protocol clear in a 1997 resolution, passed by a vote of 95-0 shortly after the convention. Senators vowed to oppose the agreement unless it required developing countries to reduce greenhouse emissions during the same time period as mandated for industrialized nations. They pointed out that developing nations, especially India and China, are rapidly increasing their use of fossil fuels.

The Senate resolution also demanded that any agreement on halting global warming include a system of "emissions credits" that would enable industrialized nations to purchase from one another the right to pollute, and an "emission trading" system that would give industrialized nations the right to pollute in exchange for helping developing nations reduce their emissions.

Business leaders assert that the requirements of the Kyoto Protocol would cost jobs and may throw the U.S. economy into a recession. "The full implementation of this treaty would cost millions of American jobs, sending industries to countries like Mexico, India, and China, who are not bound by the treaty," stated Bill Kovacs, the U.S. Chamber of Commerce's vice president for environmental policy in a news report of November 12, 1998. "This treaty should not be implemented until we are sure that the science is clear, the economic impact is mitigated and all nations are party to the agreement," Kovacs continued.

Talks in the Hague end in stalemate

In November 2000, delegates from more than 180 countries met in the Hague, The Netherlands, with the goal of implementing the Kyoto accord. They sought to develop a method for monitoring greenhouse gas emissions and to devise penalties for countries that did not reduce their emissions.

The two-week-long meeting, however, ended without an agreement. The talks broke down over a demand by the United States and some other industrialized nations to receive credit for carbon dioxide "sinks"—forested land, farmland, and other areas covered with vegetation that naturally absorb carbon dioxide. The credits would have partially offset the amount by which those nations were required to cut their emissions.

French President Jacques Chirac at the U.N. Framework Convention on Climate Change.

Opposition to the credits was voiced by New Zealand delegate Pete Hodgson. "Our concern," stated Hodgson in a November 24, 2000, newspaper article, "is that the rules would allow countries to selectively count credits for land use projects or activities that deliver no new benefit to the atmosphere."

Negotiators proposed to hold new talks on the matter, possibly in the spring of 2001. "We will not give up," stated Frank E. Loy, top negotiator for the United States in a news report of November 26, 2000. "The stakes are too high, the science too decisive, and our planet and our children too precious."

A delegate at the Climate Change Convention in the Hague. REPRODUCED BY PERMISSION OF REUTERS NEWMEDIA/CORBIS-BETTMANN.

Technology connection

Numerous forms of energy and transportation have been developed in recent decades that demonstrate that it is possible for our industrialized society to function with a minimum of environmental impact. Automobiles, the primary emitters of greenhouse gases, have been made cleaner in recent years, and vehicles that run entirely on electricity or a combination of gasoline and electricity (hybrid cars) are also now available. Solar power and wind power have been proven to be clean, safe, environmentally harmless alternatives to fossil fuels. In the United States in 1998, solar and wind power—together with hydroelectric power (power produced by moving water)—accounted for approximately 8 percent of energy consumption. Fossil fuels and nuclear power made up the other 92 percent.

Cleaner cars

Cars are responsible for one-third to one-half of all emissions causing global warming—not to mention smog and other forms of pollution. Auto manufacturers in recent years have been subjected to laws and public pressure demanding they create cleaner cars. As a result, the engines developed for 1999 and 2000 model cars put out just a small fraction of the pollutants of older engines.

Auto manufacturers are also producing electric vehicles (cars that run on batteries and electric motors instead of gasoline), hybrid vehicles (cars that run on more than one source of power, such as gasoline and electricity), and vehicles powered by fuel cells (devices that generate electricity by combining hydrogen and oxygen). Offsetting this progress, at least partially, is the recent increase in purchases of sport-utility vehicles (SUVs). SUVs, which are classified as light trucks, emit five times more pollution than cars.

Solar power

Solar radiation is the most plentiful, permanent source of energy in the world. Energy from the Sun is nonpolluting. It can be used directly for heating and lighting, or harnessed and used to generate electricity.

The sunlight that strikes Earth provides far more power than the world's inhabitants can use. The challenge of using solar power, how-

Solar power reflectors at Solar-1 near Barstow, California. REPRODUCED BY PERMISSION OF ROGER RESSMEYER/CORBIS-BETTMANN.

ever, is in the storage of the energy. Storage is necessary for times when the sun is not shining, such as at night and on cloudy days. In the absence of storage capabilities, solar energy alone cannot meet all of a community's energy needs—it must be supplemented by other sources of energy.

Great strides have been made in the development of solar power technologies since the early 1970s. France, Japan, Israel, the United States, and other countries are on the brink of using solar energy as a major source of power. A handful of large-scale solar power stations are operational around the world. In addition, small-scale solar power systems provide electricity to more than 250,000 households worldwide and a growing number of isolated areas and poor countries. The United States, as well as many European nations, has stated its intention to greatly increase the use of solar power in the twenty-first century.

Wind power

Wind energy is nonpolluting and inexhaustible (it can never be used up). There has been a sharp increase in the use of wind energy in recent years, both by private citizens and by electricity-producing power plants. This is due to worsening pollution from fossil fuels, combined with the development of new technologies in the field of wind energy.

Energy from the wind is harnessed and converted into electricity by wind turbines—windmill-like devices with long blades. A single wind turbine, placed in a location where winds are a fairly constant 10 to 12 miles (16 to 20 kilometers) per hour, can meet all the electricity needs of one home. Since the 1970s a series of wind turbines—each more powerful than the last—has been developed.

A "wind farm," consisting of hundreds or thousands of windmills in an area with strong winds, can provide enough electricity for an entire community. By the late 1980s, more than seventy wind farms were in place in Vermont, New Hampshire, Oregon, Montana, Hawaii, and California (the majority are in California).

By the end of 1993, wind energy was supplying electricity to 600,000 homes in the United States; 37,000 homes in Great Britain; and 120,000 homes in Denmark. Wind farms were also operational in Sweden, Holland, Spain, India, Australia, and other countries. By the end of 1996, about 6,000 megawatts of electricity was being produced by the tens of thousands of wind turbines worldwide. That amount of power could supply more than two million American homes.

In early 1999, the world leaders in wind power production were Germany, the United States, and Denmark. The amounts of power generated by those countries were, respectively, 2,583 megawatts; 1,946 megawatts; and 1,380 megawatts.

A matter of survival

There are a number of ways you can reduce your energy consumption, thereby reducing your contribution to global warming. Here are a few suggestions:

- Purchase compact fluorescent light bulbs. They use 40 percent less energy than incandescent (regular) light bulbs.

- Turn off lights when you leave a room.

- Make sure your home is well-insulated. One easy way to reduce heat loss in winter is to install plastic sheeting over your windows.

Horizontal axis wind turbines on a wind farm in Altamont Pass, California, in 1985.
REPRODUCED BY PERMISSION OF KEVIN SCHAFER/CORBIS-BETTMANN.

- Keep your thermostat below 70°F (21°C) in the winter. Wear extra clothing to keep warm.

- Shut down your computer when it is not in use.

- Convince your family to walk, ride bikes, or take public transportation instead of driving whenever possible.

- When shopping for a new appliance, look for the Energy Star™ label. That label indicates that the appliance has a high-energy efficiency.

- Use a manual lawnmower instead of one that is fueled by gasoline or electricity.

- Recycle paper, bottles, cans, and any other items accepted by recycling companies in your region, and purchase recycled paper goods.

For more information

Books

Bailey, Ronald H. *Glacier.* Alexandria, VA: Time-Life Books, 1982.

De Blij, Harm J., et al. *Nature on the Rampage.* Washington, DC: Smithsonian Institution, 1994. pp. 80–89.

Engelbert, Phillis. *The Complete Weather Resource.* Farmington Hills, MI: U•X•L, 1997.

Moran, Joseph M., and Lewis W. Morgan. *Essentials of Weather.* Englewood Cliffs, NJ: Prentice Hall, 1995.

Watt, Fiona, and Francis Wilson. *Weather and Climate.* London: Usborne Publishing Ltd., 1992.

Periodicals

Allen, Brian. "Capitol Hill Meltdown: While the Nation Sizzles, Congress Fiddles over Measures to Slow Down Future Climate Change." *Time.* (August 9, 1999): p. 56+.

Annin, Peter. "Power on the Prairie: In Minnesota, They're Harvesting the Wind." *Newsweek.* (October 26, 1998): p. 66.

Appenzeller, Tim. "Humans in the Hot Seat." *U.S. News & World Report.* (November 6, 2000): p. 54.

Begley, Sharon. "The Mercury's Rising." *Newsweek.* (December 4, 2000): p. 52.

Borenstein, Seth. "Hottest Years Ever Strengthen the Scientific Case for an Ever-Warming World." Knight-Ridder/Tribune News Service. (January 13, 2000).

Brown, Kathryn. "Invisible Energy." *Discover.* (October 1999): p. 36.

De Roy, Tui. "Caught in a Melting World." *International Wildlife*. (November/December 2000): pp. 12–19.

Dick, Jason. "Global Warming." *The Amicus Journal*. (Summer 1999): p. 13.

Duffy, James A. "Administration Signs Global Warming Agreement." Knight-Ridder/Tribune News Service. (November 12, 1998).

"Enviro-Cars: The Race Is On." *Business Week*. (February 8, 1999): p. 74.

"Fighting Global Warming with Iron at Sea." *Newsweek*. (October 23, 2000): p. 54.

"Global Warming May Be Beneficial." *USA Today Magazine*. (June 2000): p. 10.

Hanson-Harding, Alexandra. "Global Warming." *Junior Scholastic*. (November 27, 2000): p. 6.

Hebert, H. Josef. "Scientists Paint Grim View of Impact on U.S. of Global Warming." Associated Press. (June 9, 2000).

Helvarg, David. "Antarctica: The Ice Is Moving." *E*. (September 2000): p. 33.

Henson, Robert. "Hot, Hotter, Hottest: 1998 Raised the Bar for Global Temperature Leaps." *Weatherwise*. (March/April 1999): pp. 34–37.

Lawless, Jill. "Global Warming Threatens a Third of World's Habitats." Associated Press. (August 30, 2000).

Mazza, Patrick. "Global Warming Is Here!" *Earth Island Journal*. (Fall 1999): p. 14.

———. "The Invisible Hand: As Human Activity Warms the Earth, El Niño Grows More Violent." *Sierra*. (May-June 1998): p. 68+.

McKibbin, Warwick J., and Peter J. Wilcoxen. "Until We Know More About Global Warming, the Best Policy Is a Highly Flexible One." *The Chronicle of Higher Education*. (July 2, 1999): p. B4+.

Mulvaney, Kieran. "Alaska: The Big Meltdown." *E*. (September 2000): p. 36.

Nuttall, Nick. "Ganges Glacier 'Melting Fast.'" *The Times* (London). (July 20, 1999): p. 9.

Pearce, Fred. "Science: Meltdown in the Mountains." *The Independent* (London). March 31, 2000: p. 8.

Perkins, S. "Greenland's Ice Is Thinner at the Margins." *Science News*. (July 22, 2000): p. 54.

Peterson, Chester Jr. "Harvest the Wind: The Midwest Could Be the Saudi Arabia of Wind-Powered Energy." *Successful Farming*. (January 1999): p. 44+.

Revkin, Andrew C. "Treaty Talks Fail to Find Consensus in Global Warming." *The New York Times*. (November 26, 2000).

"Renewable Energy Resources." *Current Health 2*. (April 1999): p. S14.

Rosenfeld, Jeff. "Unearthing Climate." *Weatherwise*. (May 2000): p. 12.

Shilts, Elizabeth. "Harnessing a Powerful Breeze." *Canadian Geographic*. (May-June 1999): p. 20.

"The State of U.S. Renewable Power." *Mother Earth News*. (February 1999): p. 16.

Stevens, William K. "Catastrophic Melting of Ice Sheet Is Possible, Studies Hint." *The New York Times.* (July 7, 1998): p. B13.

————. "Human Imprint on Climate Change Grows Clearer." *The New York Times.* (June 29, 1999): p. 1+.

Sudetic, Chuck. "As the World Burns." *Rolling Stone.* (September 2, 1999): p. 97+.

"U.S. Signs Kyoto Pact." *Maclean's.* (November 23, 1998): p. 93.

Web sites

"Complete Text of Rio Declaration." *Agenda for Change.* [Online] http://www.igc.apc.org/habitat/agenda21/rio-dec.html (accessed February 12, 2001).

"Global Warning: Al Gore and the Apocalypse." *ABC News.com.* [Online] http://abc news.go.com/sections/world/warming/warming_intro.html (accessed February 12, 2001).

hurricane

9

A hurricane is a storm composed of a series of tightly coiled bands of thunderstorm clouds that forms over tropical waters. The storm has a well-defined pattern of rotating winds, with maximum sustained winds greater than 74 miles (119 kilometers) per hour. (Sustained winds are winds that blow continuously for at least one minute.)

Hurricanes are among the deadliest and most destructive of all natural disasters. A single strong hurricane can kill thousands of people. Fortunately, the number of deaths due to hurricanes has declined greatly in recent years (particularly in the United States) due to the development of early detection systems.

Hurricane Gilbert, 1990. REPRODUCED BY PERMISSION OF THE PURCELL TEAM/CORBIS-BETTMANN.

Words to Know

Air pressure: pressure exerted by the weight of air over a given area of Earth's surface. Also called atmospheric pressure or barometric pressure.

Anemometer: an instrument that measures wind speed.

Cumulonimbus: (pronounced cume-you-lo-NIM-bus) a tall, dark, ominous-looking cloud that produces thunderstorms. Also called thunderstorm cloud.

Cyclone: (pronounced SIGH-clone) the name for a hurricane that forms over the Indian Ocean.

Dropwindsonde: (also called dropsonde) a device that is released at a high altitude by an aircraft in order to transmit atmospheric measurements to a radio receiver as it falls.

Eye: the calm circle of low pressure that exists at the center of a hurricane.

Eye wall: the region of a hurricane immediately surrounding the eye, and the strongest part of the storm. The eye wall is a loop of thunderstorm clouds that produce heavy rains and forceful winds.

Flash flood: a sudden, intense, localized flooding caused by persistent, heavy rainfall or the failure of a levee or dam.

Flood: the overflow of water onto normally dry land.

Fossil fuels: coal, oil, and natural gas—materials composed of the remains of plants or animals that covered Earth millions of years ago and are today burned for fuel.

Global warming: the theory that the average temperatures around the world have begun to rise, and will continue to rise, because of an increase of certain gases in Earth's atmosphere. These gases are called "greenhouse gases" and include carbon dioxide, methane, nitrous oxide, and chlorofluorocarbons.

Greenhouse effect: the warming of Earth due to the presence of certain gases in the atmosphere, which let sunlight come in but don't let heat go back out into space—as if Earth was covered with a big glass greenhouse that keeps everything warm.

Hurricanes certainly deserve the title "the greatest storms on Earth." These storms are so powerful that just 1 percent of the energy in an average hurricane could be harnessed, it could supply the entire United States with electric power for a year. And the energy a hurricane unleashes in one day is the equivalent of 400 twenty-megaton hydrogen bombs.

Hurricane: a storm made up of a series of tightly coiled bands of thunderstorm clouds, with a well-defined pattern of rotating winds and maximum sustained winds greater than 74 miles (119 kilometers) per hour.

Meteorologists: scientists who study weather and climate.

Radiosonde: an instrument package carried aloft on a small helium-filled or hydrogen-filled balloon. It measures temperature, air pressure, and relative humidity from the ground to a maximum altitude of about 19 miles (30.4 kilometers) above Earth's surface.

Saffir-Simpson Hurricane Damage Potential Scale: the scale that ranks hurricanes according to their intensity, using the following criteria: air pressure at the eye of the storm, range of wind speeds, potential height of the storm surge, and the potential damage caused.

Storm surge: a wall of water, usually from the ocean, that sweeps onto shore when the eye of a hurricane passes overhead.

Storm tide: the combined heights of the storm surge and the ocean tide. If a storm surge hits a shore at the same time as a high tide, it can significantly increase the amount of flooding and damage.

Trade winds: dominant surface winds near the equator, generally blowing from east to west and toward the equator.

Tropical cyclone: any rotating weather system that forms over tropical waters.

Tropical depression: the weakest form of tropical cyclone, characterized by rotating bands of clouds and thunderstorms with maximum sustained winds of 38 miles (61 kilometers) per hour or less.

Tropical disturbance: a cluster of thunderstorms that is beginning to rotate.

Tropical storm: a tropical cyclone weaker than a hurricane, with organized bands of rotating thunderstorms and maximum sustained winds of 39 to 73 miles (63 to 117 kilometers) per hour.

Typhoon: (pronounced TIE-foon) the name for a hurricane that forms over the western North Pacific and China Sea region.

The word "hurricane" is only used for storms that form in the northern Atlantic Ocean or in the eastern Pacific Ocean, off the coasts of Mexico and Central America. Hurricanes that occur in the western North Pacific and China Sea region are called "typhoons" (pronounced TIE-foons), and those that form over the Indian Ocean are called "cyclones" (pronounced SIGH-clones). Hurricanes are called "baquiros" in the Philippines, "willy-willies" in northwest Australia, and "huracans" in the West Indies.

Sea Islands Storm strikes colony of former slaves

On the night of August 27, 1893, a fierce hurricane laid waste to the South Carolina Sea Islands off the coast of Beaufort, South Carolina. Some 2,000 (some sources claim as many as 5,000) islanders perished in the storm. Virtually all survivors on the islands were left homeless and penniless.

Most of the islands' 30,000 residents were former slaves. Prior to the Civil War (1861–1865), the slaves had worked on plantations on the islands. Near the start of the war, the plantation owners had fled, leaving behind their former slaves. The plantations were then divided and the newly freed slaves were given small pieces of land on which they grew cotton, potatoes, corn, peanuts, and rice. In the years since the end of slavery, the islanders had built thriving communities.

Victims were Gullah people

The islanders belonged to the distinctive Gullah culture—a way of life shaped by African heritage, the institution of slavery, and the physical isolation of the islands. Gullah culture is expressed in language, traditions, folklore, medicine, crafts, and food. Although the origin of the word "Gullah" is uncertain, the group may have named itself for the Gullah tribe of West Africa. Their language is based on English but includes words from various West African dialects. There are nearly 6,000 words in Gullah not found in the English language, such as *cooter* (tortoise), *goober* (peanut), *voodoo* (witchcraft), *hoodoo* (bad luck), and *gumbo* (okra).

Waves and winds cause death and destruction

The hurricane generated tides nearly 20 feet (6.1 meters) above average sea level and winds of 120 miles (193 kilometers) per hour. As seawater flowed over the islands, residents either jumped into their boats to try to ride out the storm or climbed to the tops of trees. (Unfortunately, the storm uprooted many of those trees and tossed them out to sea.) There were few points on land out of reach of the swirling sea. Even 25-foot-high (7.6-meter-high) sand dunes on one of the islands were flattened by the rushing water.

After the storm passed, survivors found a grisly scene of death and destruction. Bodies littered the beaches and marshes. Survivors buried the dead on the beach, in keeping with local custom, only to find that the bodies resurfaced with the action of successive tides.

The destruction of buildings and crops was near-total. The lucrative cotton crop, which had been scheduled for harvest just a few weeks after the hurricane, was wiped out. Most sources of fresh water had been contaminated with sea water, and virtually all animal life on the island had died.

An eyewitness account of the storm

Author Rachel Crane Mather interviewed Sea Islands hurricane survivors for her 1960 book *Port Royal Under Six Flags*. One woman, named Margaret Weary, shared the following recollection:

> I was so busy that evening cooking supper I never minded the wind and rain, nor the great roaring of the waves, till I looked out through the shutter and saw the sea all around the house. . . . Ma seized my little sister Grace, wrapped her in a blanket and ran to a neighbor's house on the hill. Brother and I . . . pressed on through the waves till we reached the house where Ma was. The water had come up all around that house too, and so we had to run to another, up on higher land, and there stayed all night.

A village of thatched houses on one of the South Sea Islands. REPRODUCED BY PERMISSION OF STEPHANIE COLASANTI/CORBIS-BETTMANN.

The Galveston Disaster

The greatest weather disaster in the history of the United States occurred on September 8, 1900. On that date, a hurricane struck Galveston, Texas—a low-lying barrier island on the Gulf of Mexico—and claimed more than 6,000 lives. Modern estimates put the death toll closer to 7,200.

Two days before the disaster, Galveston's residents had received warning from the U.S. Weather Bureau that a tropical storm had been detected near Cuba. The warning, however, carried little weight with Galveston islanders. After all, other tropical storms had come and gone, inflicting only minor damage. Galveston residents headed for the waterfront to enjoy the lively surf—unaware of the power of the storm that was about to engulf them.

On the morning of September 8, strong winds and higher-than-normal tides gave the first clues of the nature of the approaching storm. Rather than evacuating the island, however, most Galveston residents sought shelter in brick houses at higher elevations. Unfortunately, the highest point on the island at that time was only 9 feet (2.75 meters) above sea level—hardly enough protection to withstand the 20-foot-high (6-meter-high) storm surge that came ashore later in the day.

The hurricane lashed Galveston Island for several hours, starting at around 4:00 P.M. Winds of 100 miles (160 kilometers) per hour were recorded before the island's anemometer (instrument that measures wind speed) was destroyed. As buildings collapsed, the wreckage was carried inland to smash into other buildings. Many people were thrown into the water where high winds and surging water battered them with the debris. To add to the misery of the survivors, 10 inches (25 centimeters) of rain fell during the night.

Next morning we went home, but there was no house there, nor anything left. All had been washed away into the marsh, and the sedge and seaweed were piled up all around higher than my head. We saw dead cats and dogs, dead horses and hogs all along the shore, and some dead men and women and children.

Islanders could not escape storm's fury

The primary reason the hurricane took so many lives was not that it was an unusually large storm (in fact, it was an average hurricane, with winds of 120 miles [192 kilometers] per hour), but because the islanders

The following morning, people surveyed what was left of the town. The storm had leveled almost every structure within three blocks of the south shore and severely damaged many others. Ships had been picked up and carried inland, and the bridges from the mainland were destroyed. More than 7,000 residents perished.

Galveston was rebuilt with an eye toward preventing similar disasters in the future. To hold back storm surges, residents constructed a 17-foot-high (5.2 meter-high), 3-mile-long (4.8 kilometer-long) seawall facing the Gulf of Mexico. They also brought in huge quantities of sand to raise the elevation of the island.

Galveston, Texas, after a massive hurricane hit in 1900. REPRODUCED BY PERMISSION OF THE NATIONAL OCEANIC AND ATMOSPHERIC ADMINISTRATION/DEPARTMENT OF COMMERCE.

had no advance warning and no way to escape. The National Weather Service, which had issued a hurricane warning to mainlanders, could not get word to the islanders for lack of telegraph or telephone links.

Red Cross brings relief to area

News of the islanders' plight reached the mainland some two days after the hurricane. "The picture of desolation upon the Sea Islands is simply indescribable," wrote one witness. ". . . this unparalleled, sweeping annihilation has left no trace behind but universal destruction of every landmark." It took nearly a month for a large-scale assistance campaign to begin. Until that time, island residents survived mainly by eating berries.

The relief effort for the Sea Islands was coordinated by the American Red Cross, under the direction of its founder (and noted Civil War nurse) Clara Barton. Arriving in the area on September 30, Barton organized deliveries of food, clothing, medicine, and supplies to the islands. Many African American Civil War veterans also volunteered their services in the relief effort. The Red Cross hired hurricane survivors (whom they paid in extra food) to build houses, dig drainage ditches, and replant crops. By the following July, reconstruction of the Sea Islands communities was nearly complete.

Dangerous science: Whipping up a hurricane

A hurricane is made up of a series of tightly coiled rain bands of thunderstorm clouds. The rain bands spiral around an almost totally calm, low-pressure center called an eye. Surrounding the outer edge of the rain bands is a region of wispy, high-level clouds.

A single hurricane may contain hundreds of strong thunderstorms. The diameter of an average hurricane is around 350 miles (560 kilometers), while the diameter of the largest hurricanes can be as much as 900 miles (1,450 kilometers).

The hurricane's eye, on average, is 12 to 40 miles (20 to 65 kilometers) in diameter. Within the eye, winds are light and skies are

Air flow within a hurricane.

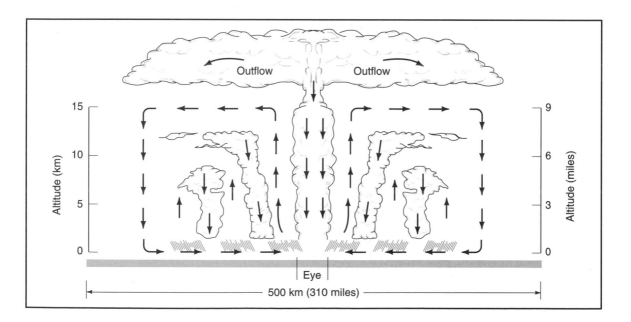

almost clear. The reason why the clouds break up in the eye of the storm is that air sinks in that region. The air warms as it falls and the moisture within it evaporates.

It may take an hour or more for the eye of the storm to pass over an area. The calm weather associated with the eye sometimes fools the residents of that area into thinking the storm is over when, in fact, the heavy winds and rain will soon resume.

The region immediately surrounding the eye, called the eye wall, is the strongest part of the storm. The eye wall is a loop of thunderstorm clouds that produce heavy rains and forceful winds. The closer one gets to the center of the storm, the faster the winds blow. Within a radius of 6 to 60 miles (10 to 100 kilometers) of the eye, winds may reach speeds of 100 to 180 miles (160 to 300 kilometers) per hour.

Formation of a hurricane according to the organized convection theory.

The winds are driven by the pressure gradient (the rate at which air pressure decreases with horizontal distance) between the edge of the storm and the eye. The closer in toward the eye, the steeper the

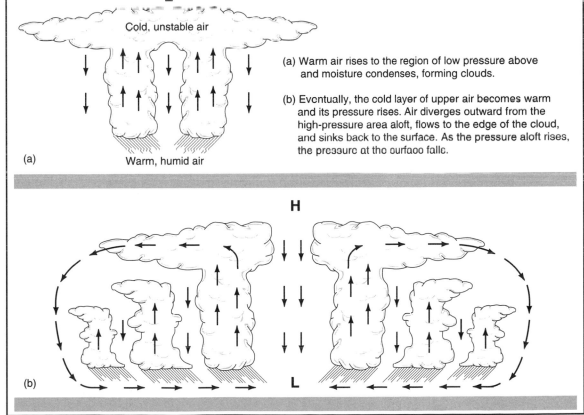

(a) Warm air rises to the region of low pressure above and moisture condenses, forming clouds.

(b) Eventually, the cold layer of upper air becomes warm and its pressure rises. Air diverges outward from the high-pressure area aloft, flows to the edge of the cloud, and sinks back to the surface. As the pressure aloft rises, the pressure at the surface falls.

Saffir-Simpson Scale: Ranking Hurricanes by Strength

The Saffir-Simpson Hurricane Damage Potential Scale places hurricanes into five categories, according to their strength. The scale was created in the early 1970s by Robert Simpson, who was the director of the National Hurricane Center at the time, and Herbert Saffir, an engineer who designed Miami's hurricane-proof building code.

According to the Saffir-Simpson Scale, Category 1 hurricanes are the weakest and Category 5 hurricanes are the strongest. A hurricane's strength is based on the air pressure at the eye of the storm, the range of wind speeds, the potential height of the storm surge, and the potential damage it will cause. The categories of potential damage are:

1) minimal

2) moderate

3) extensive

4) extreme

5) catastrophic.

A hurricane's ranking on the Saffir-Simpson Scale is increased or decreased as it goes through each of its stages of development.

Most of the hurricanes that strike the United States are Category 1 or 2. Only two hurricanes ranked as Category 3 or higher strike the United States every three years, on average.

Of the 126 tropical storms or hurricanes that hit the United States between the years 1949 and 1990, only 25 were Category 3 or higher. Those twenty-five storms, however, caused three-quarters of all property damage done by tropical storms or hurricanes during that period.

Category 5 hurricanes are the rarest kind—the United States has only experienced three of them during the twentieth century. The first was a hurricane on Labor Day, 1935 (the practice of hurricane naming did not begin until 1953), the second was Hurricane Camille in 1969, and the third was Hurricane Allen in 1980. (The hurricane that leveled Galveston, for example, would have been listed as a Category 4.)

pressure gradient becomes, and the faster the winds blow. At points farther away from the eye, the pressure gradient becomes more gradual and the winds become weaker.

The most violent part of the hurricane is the side of the eye wall, where the wind blows in the same direction that the storm is progressing. In that region, the hurricane's winds combine with the winds that are steering the hurricane, to create the storm's fastest winds.

Hurricane formation

For a hurricane to form, the air from the surface up to about 18,000 feet (5,490 meters) must be extremely humid. The air is warmed and made moist by ocean water that is at least 80°F (27°C), and remains warm to an ocean depth of about 200 feet (61 meters). The higher the temperature of the ocean water, the more water that evaporates. That, in turn, raises the humidity of the surface air. The surface air cools as it rises and the moisture within it condenses, forming clouds. When moisture condenses it releases latent heat (energy that is released or absorbed by a substance as it undergoes a phase change), which provides energy to the storm system.

Hurricane formation also requires winds at the surface of the ocean that are converging, or blowing toward a common point. Where winds converge at the surface, air rises. Winds that blow at higher altitudes must be light and be moving in approximately the same direction and speed. In that way the wind will not blow away the moist air and dissipate the developing storm.

Stages of hurricane development

A hurricane is the most intense form of a tropical cyclone. A tropical cyclone is any rotating weather system that forms over tropical waters. To qualify as a hurricane, the storm must have a well-defined pattern of rotating winds and maximum sustained winds greater than 74 miles (119 kilometers) per hour.

Less-intense forms of tropical cyclones are called tropical storms, tropical depressions, and tropical disturbances. A tropical storm is similar to a hurricane in that it has organized bands of rotating strong thunderstorms, yet it has maximum sustained winds of just 39 to 73 miles (63 to 117 kilometers) per hour. The weakest form of a tropical cyclone, a tropical depression, consists of rotating bands of clouds and thunderstorms with maximum sustained winds of 38 miles (61 kilometers) per hour or less. A tropical disturbance is a cluster of thunderstorms that is beginning to rotate. Tropical disturbances frequently occur over tropical waters. Only a small percentage of these disturbances, however, become hurricanes.

A hurricane begins as a tropical disturbance and passes through the stages of tropical depression and tropical storm on its way to maturity. A hurricane will continue to grow as long as there is a fresh supply of warm, humid air. Once the hurricane crosses over colder waters or land, its supply of warm, humid air is cut off and it weakens. A typical hurricane lasts about thirteen days. As it dissipates, a hurricane passes back through those stages of development in reverse order.

Where hurricanes form

Hurricanes only form over the warmest regions of the world's tropical oceans. The six primary hurricane-breeding regions are:

- The western North Atlantic Ocean, west of Africa and eastward to the Caribbean Sea and the Gulf of Mexico.
- The eastern Pacific Ocean, west of Mexico.
- The western portion of the North Pacific Ocean, east of China.
- The South Indian Ocean, east of Madagascar.
- The North Indian Ocean and the waters surrounding India—the Bay of Bengal and the Arabian Sea.
- The portions of the Pacific and Indian Oceans adjacent to northern and western Australia.

The world's hurricane breeding regions.

The South Atlantic and the eastern portion of the South Pacific Ocean on either side of South America, where water temperatures are cooler, are notably hurricane-free.

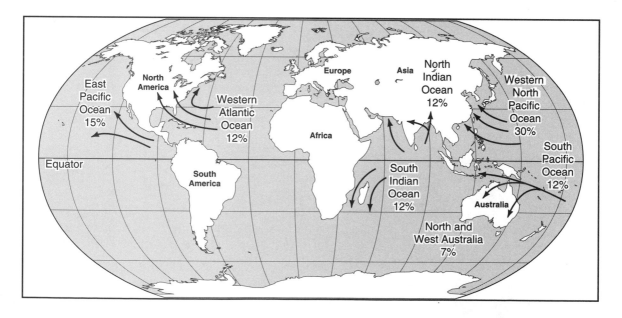

Hurricane Linda Sets a Record

Hurricane Linda, which hit in September 1997, was the strongest hurricane ever recorded in the eastern Pacific. Linda was so powerful that meteorologists proposed adding a new category, Category 6, to the Saffir-Simpson Scale (the scale presently goes up to 5). Linda packed sustained winds of 185 miles (298 kilometers) per hour with gusts greater than 200 miles (322 kilometers) per hour. By way of comparison, Hurricane Andrew, which did extensive damage to Florida in 1992 (see box), had maximum sustained winds of 140 miles (225 kilometers) per hour.

Linda's record-setting winds were measured on September 12, when the hurricane was still about 500 miles (805 kilometers) south of Mexico's Baja California Peninsula. Luckily, the hurricane followed a northwesterly route and remained at sea. The hurricane was about 1,000 miles (1,600 kilometers) west of Baja's southern tip when it broke up on September 18. Linda's only effects on land were huge waves that pounded the Baja Peninsula, the west coast of mainland Mexico, and coastal southern California.

Hurricane season

For any given location, the annual hurricane season occurs when ocean temperatures are highest. Hurricane seasons overlap with, but begin later than, the year's warmest months on land. The reason for this pattern is that it takes oceans longer to warm up (and to cool down) than it does land.

For the Northern Hemisphere, the hurricane season runs from about June 1 through November 30. In the Southern Hemisphere, hurricanes occur during the opposite six months. The exception to this rule is the western portion of the North Pacific Ocean, where hurricanes form year-round.

In each hurricane-forming region, there are peak months of hurricane development. Hurricanes in the North Atlantic region—the storms that threaten the U.S. East Coast—form in the greatest numbers in August and September.

Consequences of hurricanes

Over the ocean, a hurricane generates waves that are 50 feet (15.2 meters) or greater in height. When a hurricane washes on shore, it can bring a wall of water up to 20 feet (6 meters) high, producing severe flooding along the coast. Hurricanes also bring fierce winds and intense downpours of rain. It is not unusual for coastal and inland communities to receive 6 to 12 inches (15 to 30 centimeters) of rain when a hurricane comes onshore. Once a hurricane starts to break up over land, it may spin off numerous tornadoes that cause further damage.

While a hurricane's winds are often thought to be its most destructive element, this is not the case. It is floods—due to both the swelling of the ocean and heavy rains—that cause the most hurricane-related damage and almost 90 percent of the fatalities.

The storm surge

A storm surge is a wall of water that crashes on shore when the eye of the hurricane passes overhead. In a weak hurricane the storm surge ranges from 3 to 6.5 feet (1 to 2 meters), while in a strong hurricane it may be greater than 16 feet (5 meters). A storm surge affects up to 100 miles (160 kilometers) of coastline, leveling any structure in its path. And when squeezed into narrow channels, a storm surge produces flooding of inland bays and rivers.

Much of a storm surge's damage is caused by the debris swept along by the water. Debris may include boats that were ripped from their moorings, materials torn from buildings, trees, and sand. A storm surge also destroys structures—such as buildings, roads, and sea

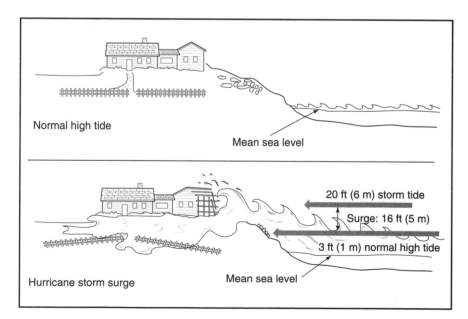

Normal high tide

Mean sea level

20 ft (6 m) storm tide

Surge: 16 ft (5 m)

3 ft (1 m) normal high tide

Mean sea level

Hurricane storm surge

A hurricane storm surge.

walls—by eroding the sand and soil beneath them, causing them to collapse.

The largest recorded storm surges occurred along the Indian Ocean and western Pacific Ocean. A storm surge estimated to be 40 feet (12 meters) struck the Bay of Bengal in 1737, killing more than 300,000 people. And in 1899, a storm surge of 42 feet (13 meters) swamped Bathurst Bay, Australia.

Winds

The winds of a hurricane—typically from 74 to 180 miles (120 to 290 kilometers) per hour—damage buildings and homes and topple trees and telephone poles, as well as cause beach erosion. A hurricane's winds can flatten lightweight structures such as mobile homes and poorly constructed buildings.

The overflowing Choluteca River, Honduras, after Hurricane Mitch in 1998. REPRODUCED BY PERMISSION OF AFP/CORBIS-BETTMAN.

Part of the wind's damage is done by objects that are picked up and hurled through the air. Shingles, aluminum siding, road signs, and other outdoor items not bolted down become deadly missiles during a

Monster Mitch

In October 1998, Hurricane Mitch became the second-deadliest Atlantic hurricane on record and the worst natural disaster in Central America in modern times. With sustained winds of 180 miles (290 kilometers) per hour and gusts greater than 200 miles (322 kilometers) per hour, Mitch tied Hurricane Camille (1969) as the fourth-strongest Atlantic hurricane of the century.

Honduras and Nicaragua—two of the poorest countries in Latin America—bore the brunt of Mitch's punishment. In Honduras Mitch claimed more than 5,600 lives. After the storm 8,000 people were missing and 1.4 million were homeless. More than 70,000 buildings were damaged or destroyed. In Nicaragua, over 3,000 people died in the hurricane, and much of the nation was reduced to a barren, mud-covered land. In all, the storm claimed approximately 9,000 lives and left some 2.4 million people homeless. It is impossible to know an exact count of people who perished in the resulting landslides and raging floodwaters.

Mitch sprang to life as a tropical storm in the southern Caribbean Sea, north of Venezuela, on October 22, 1998. Mitch then headed northwest, toward the coast of Honduras. Fueled by the warm sea water—the surface temperature at that time was 86°F (30°C)—the hurricane continued to grow. By the afternoon of October 26, Mitch had become a Category 5 ("extreme") hurricane with sustained winds of 180 miles (290 kilometers) per hour. The storm retained that strength for a record 33 hours. (The previous record for the longest time as a Category 5 storm was twenty-four hours, held jointly by Hurricane Camille [1969] and Hurricane Allen [1980].) Once Mitch

hurricane. The wind damage due to hurricanes typically occurs within 124 miles (200 kilometers) of the coast. Once a hurricane travels farther inland, it begins to weaken.

Heavy rain and flooding

A hurricane may continue to produce heavy rains and flooding for hundreds of miles inland, and for several days after the hurricane-strength winds have died down. Hurricanes typically drop 5 to 10 inches (13 to 25 centimeters) on the land, but some hurricanes have produced more than 25 inches (63 centimeters) of rain in a twenty-four-hour period.

approached to within 100 miles of shore, Honduras and Nicaragua began to experience continuous thunderstorms.

On October 28, Mitch stalled directly off the coast of Honduras, over the island of Guanaja. It remained there for two days, drenching Honduras and Nicaragua with sheets of rain and pounding the coast of Honduras with waves 40 to 50 feet (12 to 15 meters) high. At the same time, Mitch's winds stripped away every piece of vegetation on Guanaja.

On October 30, Mitch hit the coast of Honduras. It worked its way through the mountains and westward to Guatemala. The hurricane dumped as much as 25 inches (63.5 centimeters) of rain on some regions that day. Water rushed down the mountainsides, flooded the narrow valleys, and deposited a layer of mud on the flat lowlands. Banana plantations were inundated. Workers scrambled onto rooftops, where they waited out the flooding for several days. Exact rainfall totals are not known, since most rain gauges (containers that catch rain and measure the amount of rainfall) were washed away. Estimates indicate that portions of Honduras and Nicaragua received between 50 and 75 inches (127 and 190 centimeters) of rain.

As Mitch continued to journey over land it weakened, yet the rain continued throughout Central America. Five hundred people died in Mitch's floods and landslides in Guatemala and El Salvador. Roads and bridges in Guatemala were washed out, and crops were ruined.

By the time Mitch reached southeastern Mexico, it had been downgraded to a tropical depression. Mitch then headed north, toward the Yucatan Peninsula, and regained strength as it crossed the Gulf of Mexico. For Mitch's final gasp, it swept through the Florida Keys as a tropical storm with winds of 65 miles (105 kilometer) per hour. The storm spawned tornadoes that killed two people and destroyed a trailer park on Key Largo. On November 5 Mitch dumped nearly 7 inches (18 centimeters) of rain on West Palm Beach, and then headed out to sea.

When an area receives more than 6 inches (15 centimeters) of rain, flooding is likely. For some hurricanes, inland flooding turns out to be their most destructive element. For example, in 1955 Hurricane Diane brought rains and flooding to Pennsylvania, New York, and throughout New England, causing nearly 200 deaths and $4.2 billion in damage. And in 1969 Hurricane Camille dropped 9.8 inches (25 centimeters) of rain on Virginia's Blue Ridge Mountains, resulting in 150 deaths.

Tornadoes

Another category of hurricane hazards is tornadoes. About one-quarter of all hurricanes that cross over onto land in the United States produce tornadoes. A single hurricane, on average, generates ten tornadoes. The greatest number of tornadoes come from thunderstorms on a hurricane's outer region.

One theory regarding hurricane-induced tornadoes, developed by tornado specialist Theodore Tetsuya Fujita (1920–1998), states that their greatest damage is caused by small funnels called spin-up vortices. These vortices are each 9 to 30 feet (30 to 100 meters) in diameter and last only about ten seconds. In the vortices, the hurricane winds combine with the tornado winds to produce gusts of around 200 miles (320 kilometers) per hour.

The human factor

People have always settled in hurricane-prone regions. While the number of deaths due to hurricanes, particularly in the United States, has declined because of early detection systems (hurricanes currently cause 50 to 100 deaths per year in the United States), the cost of property damage by hurricanes has been steadily rising.

The effects of global warming, reportedly made worse by pollution, may be having an effect of hurricanes. The world—including the oceans—has been warming at a dramatic rate in recent years. Many scientists claim that as temperatures continue to rise, we can expect hurricanes to increase in number and size.

Theodore Fujita works with his tornado simulator.
REPRODUCED BY PERMISSION OF CORBIS-BETTMAN.

Placing ourselves in the path of danger

In the United States, people place themselves in the path of danger by settling in those areas most vulnerable to hurricane damage—the barrier islands. The barrier islands are long, narrow strips of sand that run parallel to a 2,000-mile-long (3,200-kilometer-long) Atlantic and Gulf coastline from New York to Texas. Examples of barrier islands include New York's Fire Island, Texas' Galveston Island, North Carolina's Outer Banks, and the Sea Islands off the coasts of South Carolina and Georgia. Barrier islands, which stand only 5 to 10 feet above sea level, bear the brunt of a hurricane's wind and waves and provide the mainland with a buffer from the storm. The islands respond to hurricane beatings by moving—the sand actually becomes redistributed by the waves.

Despite the fact that living on the islands is known to be dangerous, people continue to settle there. In fact, in recent years the islands have seen a huge increase in construction of housing, hotels, and businesses geared toward tourism. Drawn by the beauty of the ocean, people pay top dollar for beach residences and flock to the islands for their vacations.

Before 1940, only 10 percent of Atlantic and Gulf coast barrier islands held houses or hotels. Development steadily increased from that time. Many islands today are wholly buried under concrete and buildings.

Hurricane Fran, in 1996, wreaked havoc on the North Carolina's southeastern barrier islands. Houses, cottages, condominiums, and cars were strewn across the beach and washed out to sea. Twenty-four people died in the storm, and property damage totaled $2 billion. The following week, people began rebuilding on those islands. Barrier island development is such an attractive business proposition, in part, because U.S. taxpayers—through the National Flood Insurance Program, the Federal Emergency Management Agency's Disaster Relief Program, and the

The winds of Hurricane Beulah topple shrimp boats in Brownsville, Texas, in 1967.
REPRODUCED BY PERMISSION OF CORBIS-BETTMAN.

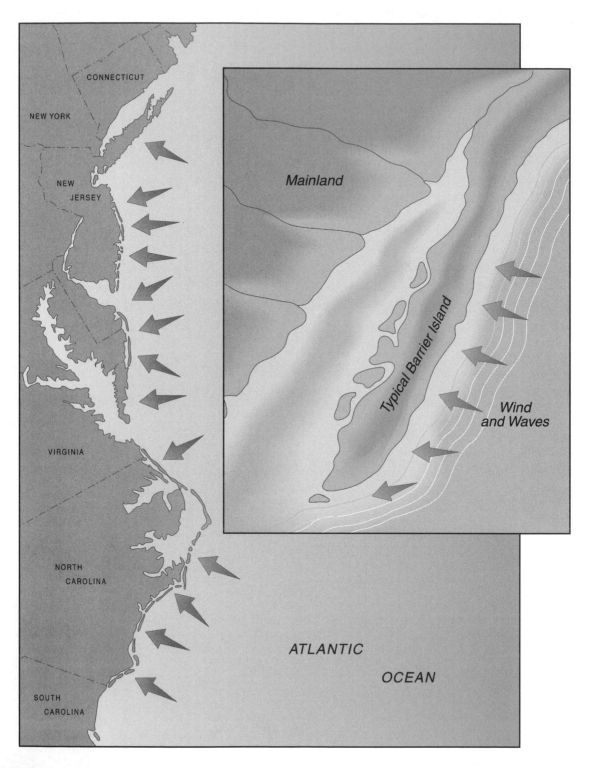

Atlantic coast barrier islands.

DANGEROUS **planet**

Army Corps of Engineers' shoreline stabilization projects—regularly pay for storm damage.

Another danger specific to barrier islands is that once a hurricane warning has been issued, evacuation is difficult. Since evacuation-route construction has not kept pace with the islands' population growth, bridges spanning the islands and the mainland become choked with traffic.

People evacuate as Hurricane Bonnie approaches Myrtle Beach, South Carolina, in 1998.
REPRODUCED BY PERMISSION OF AP/WORLD WIDE PHOTOS.

Some people have no choice

In some parts of the world, people have no choice but to live in hurricane-prone regions. Bangladesh, for instance, is a magnet for hurricanes (called cyclones in that region of the world). Its coastal region has endured seven of the nine deadliest hurricanes of the twentieth century. Bangladesh is also a densely populated, desperately poor country. For residents of the coast, moving inland would mean squeezing into already overflowing urban slums.

Global warming and hurricanes

As global warming continues and the tropical oceans heat up, hurricanes are expected to become more frequent. And since warmer water contains more fuel for hurricanes, it may give rise to storms more powerful than ever witnessed before. The world's hurricane breeding regions are expected to expand as well, as a larger area of water warms to 80°F (27°C)—the minimum water temperature necessary for hurricane formation.

Global warming is the theory that average temperatures around the world have begun to rise, and will continue to rise, due to an increase of certain gases, called greenhouse gases, in the atmosphere. The most abundant greenhouse gases are water vapor and carbon dioxide. Others include methane, nitrous oxide, and chlorofluorocarbons (CFCs) (see the chapter on Global Warming).

Technology connection

The ability of weather forecasters to warn the public of potential hurricane danger has greatly increased in recent years. Forecasters are presently able to predict, within 200 to 250 miles (320 to 400 kilometers), where a storm will be three days in the future. Forecasters at the National Hurricane Center in Miami issued their most accurate prediction yet in September 1999, when they stated that Hurricane Floyd would spare Florida and head north before striking North Carolina. As it was, Floyd missed the Florida coast by a mere 50 miles (80 kilometers).

Predictions of where a hurricane will hit land are used by public officials when calling for evacuations. Forecasters want to be as certain as possible in their predictions before recommending evacuations. If an area is evacuated only to be spared by the hurricane, residents become less likely to heed evacuation notices in the future. That attitude is perilous, since the next evacuation could be a matter of life and death. Forecasters also wish to avoid unnecessary evacuations because they are very costly. Each day of evacuation represents $1 million of lost business revenues for every mile of coastline.

Two of the most useful instruments used by hurricane researchers to detect and track tropical storms are weather aircraft and weather satellites.

Weather aircraft

Weather aircraft determine the intensity of hurricanes by probing storm clouds in upper levels of the atmosphere. They measure temper-

Gulfstream II over Los Angeles.

Ten Deadliest Hurricanes in the United States Since 1900

Note that each of the ten deadliest hurricanes in the United States occurred in the early part of the century (the most recent was in 1957). The reason for this trend is not that hurricanes used to be more ferocious, but that the death toll has been kept low in recent years due to effective advance warning systems. Also note that hurricanes were not assigned names until 1950.

Hurricane	Year	Category	Deaths
Texas (Galveston)	1900	4	6,000
Florida (Lake Okeechobee)	1928	4	1,836
Florida (Keys) and S. Texas	1919	4	600–900
New England	1938	3	600
Florida (Keys)	1935	5	408
Louisiana and Texas	1957	4	390
Louisiana (Grand Isle)	1909	4	350
Louisiana (New Orleans)	1915	4	275
Texas (Galveston)	1915	4	275

ature, air pressure, and wind speed and direction. These planes have reinforced wings and bodies, in order to withstand the hail, ice, and strong winds they encounter within the clouds. The weather instruments are carried in pods beneath the plane's wings or attached to its nose cone.

In 1996, the U.S. National Oceanic and Atmospheric Administration (NOAA) acquired a hurricane-research jet, called the Gulfstream IV-SP. The jet can cruise right through these storms at heights of up to 45,000 feet (13,725 meters). It contains sensors that measure air pressure, temperature, humidity, and wind speed at the edges and the core of the storm. It also releases hundreds of dropwindsondes (also called dropsondes)—instruments that transmit data on atmospheric conditions as they fall through the storm. The information collected by the jet is combined with readings taken at ground stations in order to better determine where a hurricane is headed.

Weather satellites

Weather satellites, which circle the globe in space, provide meteorologists with pictures and other information about hurricanes and tropical storms. The first weather satellite, launched in April 1960, was TIROS 1—Television Infrared Observation Satellite. In September 1961 weather satellites proved their value when they broadcast images of Hurricane Carla. Information from these images resulted in the nation's first widespread evacuation when 350,000 people along the Gulf coast were removed from the path of the killer hurricane.

For most people, the words "weather satellite pictures" conjure up images of swirling clouds that are seen on television newscasts. While weather satellites do produce those photos, their function is far more extensive than that. Weather satellites determine the temperature at various atmospheric levels—from the cloud tops down to the land and oceans. They also measure humidity and wind speeds in the upper air and even track plumes of invisible water vapor and relay information from one ground station to another and pick up and transmit distress signals from vessels in the air and at sea.

Today, several nations operate satellites that continuously monitor global weather.

A matter of survival

For people who live in areas affected by hurricanes, it is essential to understand and follow safety procedures. That includes making preparations before the hurricane season begins, knowing what to do when a hurricane watch or warning is issued and how to respond once a hurricane has passed.

To prepare for hurricane season, you must understand the risks that hurricanes pose to your area, learn the evacuation routes inland, and find out where emergency shelters are located. It is also crucial to develop a safety plan for your family and keep a disaster kit on hand. A kit should include the following for each person: nonperishable food; three gallons of bottled water; one change of clothing and footwear; one blanket or sleeping bag; first-aid kit; flashlight, radio, and batteries; extra set of car keys; credit card or cash; and diapers for infants.

Hurricane watches and warnings

When a hurricane threatens a coastal area, hurricane watches and warnings are issued. If it is determined that the hurricane may be life-threatening, the residents of that area are evacuated. Hurricane watches and warnings are issued by the Tropical Prediction Center (formerly the National Hurricane Center), an agency of the National Weather Service.

A hurricane watch is issued when a hurricane is headed in the general direction of an area. A watch means that hurricane conditions in the area are *possible*. Hurricane watches are announced at least thirty-six hours, and sometimes several days, in advance of an oncoming hurricane.

A hurricane warning is issued when a hurricane is poised to hit an area within twenty-four hours. A warning means that hurricane conditions are *expected* in that area. Each community within the warning area is told the probability of the hurricane's center coming within 65 miles (105 kilometers) of their community. That probability gives residents an idea of what type of damage they can expect and helps them decide whether or not to evacuate.

A hurricane warning is typically issued for a stretch of coastline 340 miles (550 kilometers) long. That stretch is about three times as large as the area that will actually be affected once a hurricane comes onshore. The reason why the warning area is so large is that it's impos-

Satellite photo of Hurricane Fran, 1996. REPRODUCED BY PERMISSION OF AP/WORLD WIDE PHOTOS.

Hurricane Andrew: The Most Expensive Natural Disaster in U.S. History

In August 1992, Hurricane Andrew struck Florida and Louisiana, causing 58 deaths and leaving 160,000 people homeless. Andrew damaged or destroyed more than 200,000 buildings, for a total of some $30 billion in damages. Andrew, which came ashore as a Category 4 hurricane, was the costliest natural disaster in U.S. history.

On August 21, Andrew was classified as a tropical storm in the Atlantic Ocean with winds of just 52 miles (84 kilometers) per hour. It then moved over warmer waters and gained strength. By August 23, Andrew had become an intense hurricane with maximum sustained winds of 140 miles (225 kilometers) per hour.

On August 24, Andrew crossed onto land at Homestead, on Florida's southern tip. With wind gusts of around 200 miles (322 kilometers) per hour and a 16.9-foot-tall storm surge (a record for Florida), Andrew tore up Homestead. The storm blew over trees, knocked down utility poles, and damaged 50,000 homes.

Andrew then traveled westward across the state and into the Gulf of Mexico. Once over the Gulf's warm waters, the hurricane regained the strength it had lost on land. On August 25, Andrew blew into Louisiana with

sible to predict the exact point at which the storm will hit land because a hurricane often changes course at the last minute.

What to do when you are within a hurricane watch area:

- Stay tuned to radio or television reports of the storm's progress.

- Fill your car with gas and get cash, if needed.

- If you live in a mobile home, make sure it's securely fastened, then evacuate.

- Cover all windows and doors with shutters or plywood.

- Check your supply of nonperishable food and water.

- Gather first-aid materials and medications.

- Bring lawn furniture, garbage cans, garden hoses, and other lightweight items inside.

winds that were recorded at 138 miles (222 kilometers) per hour, and the path of destruction continued.

Thanks to the effectiveness of storm predictions and advance warnings, Andrew's death toll was relatively low. More than 1 million people in Florida and 1.7 million people in Louisiana and Mississippi were evacuated from areas in the storm's path. Had Andrew occurred before the advent of sophisticated weather forecasting technology, the death toll certainly would have been much higher.

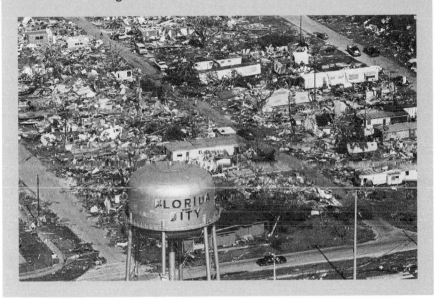

Florida City, Florida, after Hurricane Andrew in 1992. REPRODUCED BY PERMISSION OF AP/WIDE WORLD PHOTOS.

- If you have a boat, be sure it's properly secured.

- Evacuate if you live in a mobile home or high-rise, on the coastline, on an offshore island, or near a river or flood plain.

What to do when you are within a hurricane warning area:

- Stay tuned to radio or television reports of the storm's progress.

- Finish covering your windows and doors and prepare your home for evacuation.

- Evacuate immediately upon the orders of local officials and travel inland, to the home of a friend or relative, a low-rise motel, or an emergency shelter.

- Notify someone outside of the hurricane warning area of your evacuation plans.

Naming Hurricanes

Before 1950, hurricanes were primarily identified by their latitude and longitude (positions north and south, and east and west, respectively, on the globe). This method of labeling was complicated because hurricanes rapidly changed their position. It was especially confusing if there was simultaneously more than one hurricane on the same ocean.

In 1950 meteorologists began assigning names to all hurricanes and tropical storms that formed in the western portion of the North Atlantic Ocean, the Caribbean, and the Gulf of Mexico. The naming of storms in the eastern portion of the Pacific Ocean didn't begin until 1959.

From 1950 to 1953, names were taken from the international radio code words that corresponded with letters of the alphabet. For instance, the first three letters—"A," "B," and "C"—had the names Able, Baker, and Charlie.

In 1953 meteorologists began assigning female names to the storms. The names were designated in alphabetical order, starting with the "As," for each new season. ("Qs," "Us," and "Zs" were not used.) Starting in 1978 in the eastern Pacific, and in 1979 in the North Atlantic, male names, as well as names in French and Spanish, have also been used.

Hurricane names are submitted by countries that lie in the path of hurricanes for approval by the Region 4 Hurricane Committee of the World Meteorological Organization. (Region 4 is composed of representatives of countries affected by hurricanes.)

Names are assigned in advance for six-year cycles. At the end of six years, the names may be re-used. The names of hurricanes that cause extensive damage—such as Camille, Gilbert, Gloria, Hugo, Mitch, and Andrew—are removed from the list for at least ten years—and in some cases, they are removed permanently.

Presently, each hurricane-producing region of the world (except the North Indian Ocean, where cyclones are not named) has its own lists of names, drawn up years in advance. Each storm is automatically assigned the next name on the list.

On the following page is a list of hurricane names for the Atlantic Ocean and the eastern portion of the North Pacific Ocean for the years 2000 through 2004.

Atlantic Ocean Names:

2000	2001	2002	2003	2004
Alberto	Allison	Arthur	Ana	Alex
Beryl	Barry	Bertha	Bill	Bonnie
Chris	Chantal	Cristobal	Claudette	Charley
Debby	Dean	Dolly	Danny	Danielle
Ernesto	Erin	Edouard	Erika	Earl
Florence	Felix	Fay	Fabian	Frances
Gordon	Gabrielle	Gustav	Grace	Gaston
Helene	Humberto	Hanna	Henri	Hermine
Isaac	Iris	Isidore	Isabel	Ivan
Joyce	Jerry	Josephine	Juan	Jeanne
Keith	Karen	Kyle	Kate	Karl
Leslie	Lorenzo	Lili	Larry	Lisa
Michael	Michelle	Marco	Mindy	Matthew
Nadine	Noel	Nana	Nicholas	Nicole
Oscar	Olga	Omar	Odette	Otto
Patty	Pablo	Paloma	Peter	Paula
Rafael	Rebekah	Rene	Rose	Richard
Sandy	Sebastien	Sally	Sam	Shary
Tony	Tanya	Teddy	Teresa	Tomas
Valerie	Van	Vicky	Victor	Virginie
William	Wendy	Wilfred	Wanda	Walter

Eastern Portion of the North Pacific Ocean Names:

2000	2001	2002	2003	2004
Aletta	Adolph	Alma	Andres	Agatha
Bud	Barbara	Boris	Blanca	Blas
Carlotta	Cosme	Cristina	Carlos	Celia
Daniel	Dalila	Douglas	Dolores	Darby
Emilia	Erick	Elida	Enrique	Estelle
Fabio	Flossie	Fausto	Felicia	Frank
Gilma	Gil	Genevieve	Guillermo	Georgette
Hector	Henriette	Hernan	Hilda	Howard
Ileana	Israel	Iselle	Ignacio	Isis
John	Juliette	Julio	Jimena	Javier
Kristy	Kiko	Kenna	Kevin	Kay
Lane	Lorena	Lowell	Linda	Lester
Miriam	Manuel	Marie	Marty	Madeline
Norman	Narda	Norbert	Nora	Newton
Olivia	Octave	Odile	Olaf	Orlene
Paul	Priscilla	Polo	Patricia	Paine
Rosa	Raymond	Rachel	Rick	Roslyn
Sergio	Sonia	Simon	Sandra	Seymour
Tara	Tico	Trudy	Terry	Tina
Vicente	Velma	Vance	Vivian	Virgil
Willa	Wallis	Winnie	Waldo	Winifred
Xavier	Xina	Xavier	Xina	Xavier
Yolanda	York	Yolanda	York	Yolanda
Zeke	Zelda	Zeke	Zelda	Zeke

- If you have pets that you are unable to take with you, leave them plenty of food and water.

If you are staying at home:

- Fill the bathtub and containers with drinking water, unplug small appliances, turn off propane tanks, and turn your refrigerator to its coldest possible setting.

- In case of strong winds, close all outside and inside doors and go into a small interior room or hallway on the first floor, away from windows and doors. If possible, crouch beneath a sturdy piece of furniture.

What to do after the hurricane:

- Stay tuned to the radio or television for information.

- Don't return home until your area has been declared safe.

- Don't attempt to drive around a barricade; if you encounter one, turn around and take a different route.

- Don't drive on roads or bridges in flooded areas or on washed-out roads.

- Inspect your gas, water, and electrical lines for damage before using.

- Be sure that your tap water is not contaminated before drinking or cooking with it.

- Make as few calls as possible so you don't tie up phone lines.

For more information

Books

Ahrens, C. Donald. *Meteorology Today: An Introduction to Weather, Climate, and the Environment*. 5th ed. St. Paul, MN: West Publishing Company, 1994.

Allen, Leslie, et. al. *Raging Forces: Earth in Upheaval*. Washington, DC: National Geographic Society, 1995.

Anthes, Richard A. *Meteorology*, 6th ed. New York: Macmillan Publishing Company, 1992.

Burroughs, William J., Bob Crowder, et. al. *Nature Company Guides: Weather*. New York: Time-Life Books, 1996.

Christian, Spencer. *Spencer Christian's Weather Book*. New York: Prentice-Hall, 1993.

Fisher, David E. *The Scariest Place on Earth: Eye to Eye with Hurricanes*. New York: Random House, 1994.

Gemmell, Kathy. *Storms and Hurricanes*. London, England: Usborne Publishing Ltd., 1995.

Kahl, Jonathan D. W. *Weather Watch: Forecasting the Weather*. Minneapolis, MN: Lerner Publications Company, 1996.

Larsen, Erik. *Isaac's Storm*. New York: Crown Publishers, 1999.

Lauber, Patricia. *Hurricanes: Earth's Mightiest Storms*. New York: Scholastic Press, 1996.

Lee, Sally. *Hurricanes*. New York: Franklin Watts, 1993.

Moran, Joseph M., and Lewis W. Morgan. *Essentials of Weather*. Englewood Cliffs, NJ: Prentice Hall, 1995.

Robinson, Andrew. *Earth Shock: Hurricanes, Volcanoes, Earthquakes, Tornadoes and Other Forces of Nature*. New York: Thames and Hudson, 1993.

Watt, Fiona, and Francis Wilson. *Weather and Climate*. London, England: Usborne Publishing Ltd.: 1992.

Williams, Jack. *The Weather Book: An Easy-to-Understand Guide to the USA's Weather*. New York: USA Today & Vintage Books, 1992.

Periodicals

Ackerman, Jennifer. "Islands at the Edge." *National Geographic*. (August 1997): pp. 2–31.

Beardsley, Tim. "Dissecting a Hurricane." *Scientific American*. (March 2000): pp. 80–85.

Bentley, Mace, and Steve Horstmeyer. "Monstrous Mitch." *Weatherwise*. (March/April 1999): pp. 15–18.

Black, Harvey. "Hurricanes: Satellite Enhancements." *Weatherwise*. (Feb./March 1996): pp. 10 11.

Cobb, Jr., Charles E. "Bangladesh: When the Water Comes." *National Geographic*. (June 1993): pp. 118–134.

Fox, Stephen. "For a While . . . It Was Fun." *Smithsonian*. (September 1999): pp. 128–130, 132, 134–140, 142.

Gore, Rick. "Andrew Aftermath." *National Geographic*. (April 1993): pp. 2–37.

Henson, Robert. "The Intensity Problem: How Strong Will a Hurricane Get?" *Weatherwise*. (September/October 1998): pp. 20–26.

"Hurricane Havoc in Central America." *The Economist*. (November 7, 1998): p. 33.

"Hurricanes Rip Through Impoverished Caribbean, Central American Regions." *National Catholic Reporter*. (November 20, 1998): p. 12.

Iocavelli, Debi. "Hurricanes: Eye Spy." *Weatherwise*. (Aug./Sept. 1996): pp. 10–11.

Le Comte, Douglas. "Weather Highlights: Around the World 1997." *Weatherwise*. (March/April 1998): pp. 26–31.

"Murderous Mitch." *Time*. (November 16, 1998): p. 66.

Rosenfeld, Jeff. "The Forgotten Hurricane." *Weatherwise*. (Aug./Sept. 1993): pp. 13–18.

"Troubled on the Sea Islands." *Scholastic Update*. (September 20, 1996): p. 15+.

U.S. Dept. of Commerce. *Hurricanes—The Greatest Storms on Earth*. Washington: NOAA, 1994.

Williams, A. R. "After the Deluge." *National Geographic.* (November 1999): pp. 108–129.

Williams, Jack. "Watching the Vapor Channel: Satellites Put Forecasters on the Trail of Weather's Hidden Ingredient." *Weatherwise.* (Aug./Sept. 1993): pp. 26–30.

Web sites

"Billion Dollar U.S. Weather Disasters, 1980–1996." *National Climatic Data Center.* [Online] http://www.ncdc.noaa.gov/ (accessed on March 8, 2001).

"Global Warming: Al Gore and the Apocalypse." *ABC News.com.* [Online] http://abcnews.go.com/sections/world/warming/warming_evidence.html (accessed on March 8, 2001).

"Hurricane Names." *FEMA for Kids.* [Online] http://www.fema.gov/kids/hunames.htm (accessed on March 8, 2001).

"1998: A 'Mean' Season for Atlantic Hurricanes." *National Oceanic and Atmospheric Administration.* [Online] http://www.outlook.noaa.gov/98hurricanes/ (accessed on March 8, 2001).

"Relief Efforts Following the Sea Islands Hurricane (1893)." *African Americans in the American Red Cross.* [Online] http://www.redcross.org/museum/vmuseum/aaexhibit/seaisrlf.html (accessed on March 8, 2001).

"The Sea Islands Hurricane of 1893." *National Oceanic and Atmospheric Administration.* [Online] http://wchs.csc.noaa.gov/1893.htm (accessed on March 8, 2001).

Stormfax Weather Almanac. [Online] http://www.stormfax.com/ (accessed on March 8, 2001).

USA Today Weather. [Online] http://www.usatoday.com/weather/wfront.htm (accessed on March 8, 2001).

The Weather Channel. [Online] http://www.weather.com/ (accessed on March 8, 2001).

"World-Wide Tropical Cyclone Names." *National Hurricane Center.* [Online] http://www.nhc.noaa.gov/aboutnames.html (accessed on March 8, 2001).

landslide

A landslide is the movement of large amounts of soil, rocks, mud, and other debris downward along a slope. The movement is caused by the pull of gravity and occurs when a mountainside or hillside weakens and is unable to support its own weight. The amount of material that falls in a landslide can be as small as the size of a refrigerator or as large as an entire mountainside. The falling material can move slowly or quickly, and may travel a few feet (meters) or several miles (kilometers) before it stops. Some landslides move only a little each year. Such movement may be irregular, or it may happen at the same time each year, such as in the spring, when the snow melts.

Landslide approaching farm buildings in California. REPRODUCED BY PERMISSION OF JLM VISUALS.

Words to Know

Debris avalanche: a downward slide of loose, earthen material (soil, mud, and small rocks) that begins suddenly and travels at great speeds—similar to a snow avalanche. It builds into a fearsome mass of mud, trees, and rocks that can cause much damage.

Debris slide: a slide of small rocks and shallow layers of loose soil that commonly follows volcanic eruptions.

Deforestation: the removal of all or most of the trees from a region.

Earthflow: a landslide that consists of material that is moist and full of clay, yet drier than the material in mudflows.

Earthquake: a sudden shifting of masses of rock beneath Earth's surface, which releases enormous amounts of energy and sends out shock waves that cause the ground to shake.

Erosion: the removal of soil by water or wind. This is especially harmful when the top layer of soil, called the topsoil, is stripped away, because this is the layer where plants grow.

Fall: the downward motion of rock or soil through the air or along the surface of a steep slope.

The most common cause of landslides is excessive moisture in the ground, because of heavy rains or melting snow. When the ground becomes so full of water it cannot hold any more, the soil loses its ability to stick together. It also becomes heavier, which hastens its movement down the slope. The cause of the largest and most devastating landslides is earthquakes. Other events that trigger landslides include volcanoes and vibrations from explosions or heavy traffic. Human activities, such as mountainside development and mining also contribute to instability on slopes. Forest fires are indirect causes of landslides, since they remove the vegetation and roots that hold the soil in place.

While rapid landslides cause the greatest loss of life and property, even slow landslides can cause structural damage to buildings and rupture underground power lines and water mains. Each year in the United States, landslides cause between twenty-five and fifty deaths and up to $2 billion in damage. In less-developed nations—where there are often less-strict zoning laws (allowing construction in landslide-prone areas), higher population densities, and a lack of protective structures—the death tolls and amount of property damage are much higher.

Lahar: (pronounced LAH-hahr) a mudflow composed of volcanic ash and water that occurs in the wake of a volcanic eruption.

Landslide: the movement of large amounts of soil, rocks, mud, and other debris downward and outward along a slope.

Mudflow: a landslide consisting of soil mixed with water. It is wetter than the material in an earthflow.

Rockslide: a cascade of rocks (of any size) down a steep slope at high speeds.

Saturated: containing the maximum amount of water a material can hold.

Slump: the slow downhill movement of large portions (called blocks) of a slope. Each block rotates backward toward the slope in a series of curving movements.

Solifluction: (pronounced so-lih-FLUC-shun) the most rapid type of earthflow, occurring when snow or ice thaws or when earthquakes produce shocks that turn the soil into a fluid mass.

Volcano: an opening in Earth's surface through which gases, hot rocks, and ash are ejected from the heated inner portion of the planet.

The Frank Slide

In the early morning hours of April 29, 1903, a block of limestone approximately 0.5 square mile (0.8 square kilometer) in area cascaded onto the coal-mining village of Frank in south-central Alberta, Canada. The limestone, which weighed 50 million to 90 million tons (45 million to 82 million metric tons) and was 500 feet (152 meters) thick, came hurtling down from a height of 3,100 feet (945 meters) between two peaks of Turtle Mountain. Seventy-six people were killed instantly in the landslide, although some records place the number as high as ninety. In addition to burying part of the town, the fallen rock dammed the Crowsnest River and created a new lake.

Native inhabitants feared the mountain

The native people, who were the original inhabitants of the region, recognized the dangers of Turtle Mountain. The mountain had been named for its shape, which resembled a turtle's shell and had a slab of limestone sticking out like a turtle's head. To the Indians, it was "the mountain that walked." Fearing a rockslide, the native people shunned the idea of settling, or even so much as camping, at the base of the mountain.

Turtle Mountain was indeed geologically unstable, meaning it had little resistance to sliding or collapsing. The twin-peaked mountain was composed of weather-worn limestone toward its peak and soft stone laced with veins of coal at lower altitudes. The angle of the mountain was especially steep on the eastern slope, and the face had developed cracks. Along the cracks, the rock was fragmented. An earthquake two years prior to the rockslide had made the rock fragmentation worse. Further weakening of the rock foundation was brought about by the tunneling of coal mining shafts, which were dug about 1 mile (1.3 kilometers) into the mountain.

Frank established as a mining town

The town of Frank was incorporated on September 10, 1901, just eleven months after a coal deposit had been discovered at the base of the mountain. It was named after H. L. Frank, a banker from Montana, who had funded a mining operation to extract the coal. He persuaded adventurous frontiersmen—many of them recent arrivals from Europe—to travel to Turtle Mountain and work in the mine. He also paid the Canadian Pacific Railway to run railroad tracks from the main line to the mine entrance. By the time the town of Frank was established, miners were extracting hundred of tons (metric tons) of coal each day.

The town of Frank looked just like a Hollywood set for a western movie. Among the company buildings—miner's cabins, office buildings, and a boarding house—sprang up hotels, saloons, and casinos. The miners spent a significant portion of their earnings on drinking and gambling. By the spring of 1903, Frank had a population of approximately 600.

The mountain tumbles down

In the months prior to the landslide, miners had reported numerous sounds that should have been taken as warnings of the mountain's instability. The wooden supports in the tunnels groaned loudly and the tunnel walls shook. The vibrations had become so violent that coal literally dropped from the ceiling, forming piles that the miners merely had to shovel into cars. The night before the landslide, the mountain emitted a rumble that could be heard throughout the valley. Area residents ignored the noise and went to sleep.

Disaster struck at 4:10 A.M. the next morning. According to Sid Choquette, a brakeman on the railroad who had been walking alongside a slow-moving train, the mountain began to creak and groan loudly, then emitted an eerie whistling roar. Next Choquette heard a sound like cannon fire and saw a huge slab of rock racing down the slope, right toward the town. Choquette jumped aboard the train and the engineer set the controls on full-throttle. The train raced for the bridge that spanned the

Crowsnest River and made it across just moments before the avalanche of rocks wiped out the bridge. The railroad crew watched, stunned, as millions of tons (metric tons) of limestone plowed through the south side of Frank, continued 2.5 miles (3.2 kilometers) across the valley floor, and then climbed 400 feet (122 meters) up the opposite slope.

In a little more than a minute the rockslide, plus a wall of cold air that forcefully thrust ahead of it, leveled much of the town of Frank, killing many of its residents. Three-quarters of the houses were destroyed, as were the electric power plant, the livery stable, the shoe store, the miners' temporary quarters, the construction camp, the cemetery, and more than one mile of the Canadian Pacific Railroad. The debris tumbled into the river, blocking the flow of water, and portions of the railroad tracks were covered by rocks 100 feet (30 meters) deep. Structures were ripped apart, flung across the valley, and then buried forever by the massive limestone boulders. Only twelve bodies were recovered, and the exact number of dead was never determined. Because there were no accurate records of the number of inhabitants at the time, it was impossible to compile a list of the missing.

Trapped miners dig themselves out

When the rocks fell, seventeen workers were inside the mine and three others were taking a lunch break outside the entrance. The rockslide fell on the entrance, killing the three men outside and trapping the others inside. The miner most familiar with the mine's layout informed his trapped co-workers that they were at least 295 feet (90

The Frank Slide Interpretive Center near the site of a 1903 rockslide that buried the town of Frank in Alberta, Canada. REPRODUCED BY PERMISSION OF DAVID G. HOUSER/CORBIS-BETTMANN.

meters) from the edge of the mountain. The miners knew they had to act quickly if they were going to get out alive. They realized the airshafts were probably blocked, meaning that breathable air would be in short supply. They were also concerned that explosive and lethal gases might be escaping from cracks in the rock walls.

The miners first tried to tunnel outward, but made little progress. Every time they dug into the wall, more rock tumbled down to fill in the space. After a few hours they tried a new strategy: digging upward, along a vein of coal. The coal was softer and easier to remove than the limestone. Three men dug at a time. They worked in shifts, making slow but steady progress. About thirteen hours after the rockslide, the miners reached the surface. They climbed out onto the mountainside and looked in horror upon the devastation below.

Rescue efforts

People in Frank not directly in the rockslide's path were shaken from their slumber by the loud roar. Stunned, they staggered into the streets to see what had happened. Seeing fires and hearing screams for help, some people grabbed their lanterns and rushed toward the wreckage. The avalanche, however, spared few of those it touched. Rescuers only found twenty-three people alive in the landslide's path.

At one ruined home, merchant Alex Leitch, along with his wife and four sons, were found dead. At another home, Sam Ennis had dug himself out of the rubble and worked with rescuers to free his wife, Lucy, from a beam that had fallen on her. Even while trapped, Lucy Ennis had managed to save her baby daughter, Gladys, who was choking on a clod of dirt. Sam Ennis's brother-in-law, James Warrington, was also buried beneath a pile of rocks. Warrington warned rescuers to dig gingerly, since he felt something soft beneath him. It turned out that Warrington had landed on top of his next-door neighbor, Mrs. Watkins, who had been thrown from her own house.

On the railroad tracks, brakeman Sid Choquette, still shaken from his near-miss with death, turned his attention to the passenger train that was due to arrive in an hour. If it wasn't warned, the train would crash into the rock-covered tracks. He made his way through the cloud of dust that hung in the air and across rocks the size of small buildings until he arrived at the tracks on the east side of the rockpile. With only minutes to spare, he was able to flag down the train and prevent a second disaster.

The aftermath of the slide

It was later determined that the slide had been set in motion when a sudden cold spell caused water from melting snow to freeze within the cracks. The freezing water had expanded as it turned to ice and had forced the cracks to widen, sending the rocks tumbling down the slopes.

The mine reopened briefly after the landslide, only to be shut down by a fire in 1905. H. L. Frank suffered a nervous breakdown and was placed in a mental institution; he died there in 1908. The mine reopened one more time, but was permanently closed in 1918. Today, about 200 people live in the town of Frank.

Dangerous science: How landslides happen

Landslides are classified into three groups: slides, falls, and flows, depending upon the type of material, the amount of air and water it contains, and the speed with which it falls.

Slides

A slide consists of rock, mud, soil, water, or debris—or any combination of those materials—that goes tumbling down a steep slope at

Rescue workers removing body from mudslide in Ginebra, Colombia.

Mudflows Strike Southern Italy

Two days of heavy rains set off deadly mudflows in the Campania region of Southern Italy on May 5, 1998. The rivers of mud that rushed down from the mountains flowed into several towns across a 35-mile-wide (60-kilometer-wide) stretch from Sarno to Naples. One week after the disaster the death toll was put at 139, with an estimated 146 people still missing. The majority of the fatalities occurred in Sarno (population 2,000).

The mudflows were so forceful that they inundated buildings, destroyed homes, and buried people. At least 1,500 people were left homeless. In the wake of the disaster, the streets of the affected towns were wastelands of mud, wood, boulders, and other debris. Telephone, electricity, and water service were cut off. The mudflows were among Italy's worst natural disasters of all times; they were nicknamed by the Italian media the "Pompei of the Year 2000," after the famous volcanic eruption that took thousands of lives in A.D. 79.

"I heard an incredible noise," stated survivor Francesca Bonaiuto of Sarno, in a CNN Online news story of May 7, 1998. "It sounded like the mountain coming down on us. My husband said 'let's get the car.' I said, 'no, just run.' If we had taken the car, we never would have made it." Bonaiuto's aunt and uncle died in the mudflow.

Several thousand soldiers, firefighters, and military personnel from a nearby U.S. Navy base quickly arrived on the scene and searched for survivors. They freed several people trapped in homes or cars. In one notable rescue, searchers found a man who, for three days, had been buried up to his neck in mud in his cellar. Rescue workers used bulldozers and shovels to clear streets of hardened mud, which in some places was stacked 10 feet (3 meters) high.

The damage from the mudslide was blamed on lax construction codes, which allowed the building of houses in areas known to be vulnerable to mudslides. Another factor was the illegal building of houses in areas where construction had been placed off-limits. The intensity of the mudslides was due, in part, to recent forest fires that had stripped the slopes of vegetation.

Vehicles buried by mud in Boulder Creek, California.
REPRODUCED BY PERMISSION OF JIM SUGAR PHOTOGRAPHY/ CORBIS-BETTMANN.

high speeds. A slide typically destroys everything in its path before finally coming to rest on a plateau or in the valley below. Rockslides are common in the European Alps, the U.S. Appalachians, and the Canadian Rockies, especially on slopes with few trees. They are frequently triggered by heavy rains, but can occur at any time without an obvious cause. Debris slides, made up of small rocks and shallow layers of loose soil, commonly follow volcanic eruptions.

A debris avalanche—a particularly dangerous variety of slide—begins suddenly and travels at speeds as fast as hundreds of miles (kilometers) per hour. Debris avalanches, which resemble their snowy cousins (see the chapter on Avalanches), occur most frequently on mountains in humid climates. They begin when soil at the top of a slope becomes saturated with water. That material begins to slide downward, building into a fearsome mass of mud, trees, rocks, and anything else in its path. A debris avalanche that occurred in 1977 in the Peruvian Andes, for example, contained between 20 million and 45 million cubic yards (15 million and 34 million cubic meters) of material traveling at about 100 miles per hour. The debris fell upon a city in the foothills, killing some 19,000 people.

Falls

A fall involves rock or soil dropping from an overhanging cliff or a steep slope. The most dangerous type of fall is a rockfall. Huge boulders may fall freely through the air or race down a mountainside, fragmenting into small pieces as they descend and becoming a raging current of debris. Rockfalls typically occur where cliffs have become steepened by erosion from rivers, glaciers, or waves. The rocks may be pried loose from the cliff or mountain by the freezing and thawing of water in the slope's cracks. Evidence of rockfalls can be seen in the piles of rock and debris at the base of steep slopes.

Large rockfalls can cause terrific damage. In 1970, for instance, a rockfall from the peak of the Huascarán volcano in Peru, triggered by an earthquake, created a debris avalanche that buried villages at the base of the volcano and killed almost 20,000 people (see the Avalanche chapter).

A geologist who witnessed the 1970 rockfall reported:

I heard a great roar coming from Huascarán. Looking up, I saw what appeared to be a great cloud of dust and it looked as though a large mass of rock and ice was breaking loose from the north peak. . . . The crest of the wave [of rock and ice] had a curl, like a huge breaker coming in from the ocean. I estimated the wave to be at least 80 meters [260 feet] high. I observed hundreds of people in

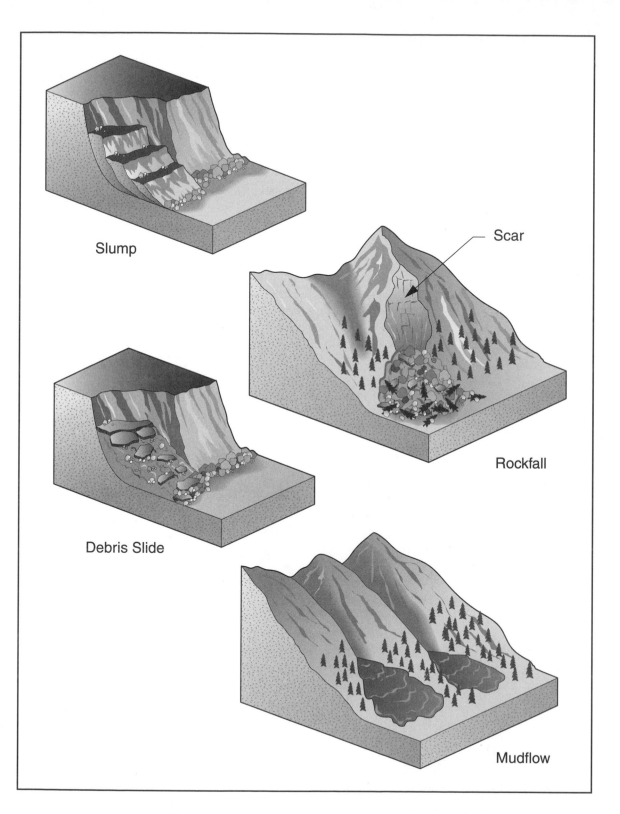

Slump

Scar

Rockfall

Debris Slide

Mudflow

DANGEROUS **planet**

Yungay running in all directions and many of them towards Cemetery Hill. All the while, there was a continuous loud roar and rumble. I reached the upper level of the cemetery near the top just as the debris flow struck the base of the hill and I was probably only ten seconds ahead of it. . . . It was the most horrible thing I have ever experienced and I will never forget it.

Flows

A flow is a landslide of wet material, which may contain rock, soil, and debris, combined with water. Mudflows are the most common, most liquid, and fastest type of flow. They contain water and soil, with a consistency somewhere between soup and freshly poured concrete.

Mudflows frequently occur in dry or semi-dry mountains and on steep-sided volcanoes that receive sudden, heavy rainfall. Loose, weathered rock and steep slopes with little or no vegetation are prone to mudflows. Mudflows can travel as fast as 55 miles (88 kilometers) per hour and have enough force to pick up and carry along debris the size of boulders, cars, trees, and houses. They typically spread out across great distances on valley floors, depositing a thin layer of mud mixed with boulders. In the United States mudflows do millions of dollars of damage every year. One region vulnerable to mudflow damage is Southern California, especially the hilly suburban communities.

Another type of flow, called an earthflow, consists of material that is moist and full of clay, yet drier than the material in mudflows. Earthflows are most often set in motion by heavy rains and move at a variety of speeds and distances, yet are generally slower and travel shorter distances than mudflows. Slow earthflows creep along, stopping and starting, moving sometimes just several feet per year. They are common on hillsides on the California coast where the soil has a high clay content.

A type of earthflow that occurs on slopes at high elevations and in polar regions is solifluction (pronounced so-lih-FLUC-shun; also called soil fluction; this action is not included in narrow definitions of landslide). Solifluction involves sensitive layers of silt and clay that underlie level terraces. It takes place, at speeds ranging from very slow to very fast, when snow or ice thaws or when earthquakes produce shocks that turn the soil into a fluid mass. This flow of watery sediment is common in Scandinavia and on the slopes above the St. Lawrence River valley in Quebec, Canada. In 1971, a solifluction earthflow at St.-Jean Vianney in the St. Lawrence River valley swept away thirty-eight homes and took thirty-one lives.

There are also earthflows of dry-material that move very quickly, sometimes for great distances, over gentle slopes. Dry-material earthflows

Opposite page:
Types of landslide.

can be triggered by earthquakes or the falling of rock from steep slopes above. An earthquake in 1920 in the Gansu (formerly Kansu) province in China set into motion the massive flow of dry loess (pronounced LOW-ess; wind-deposited silt), which resulted in the deaths of tens of thousands of people (see the box on Gansu landslide on page 273).

Slumps

A slump, which is included in broad definitions of landslide, is the slow, downhill movement—7 feet (2 meters) per day or slower—of portions of a slope. Slumps take place on slopes where there is a strong surface layer of rock or sediment and a weaker layer of material underneath. When the lower layer is no longer able to support the surface material, both layers slip downward together. A slump may range in size from a few square yards (square meters) to thousands of square yards (square meters). As the ground moves, it tilts, or rotates, backward toward the slope in a series of curving downward and outward movements. On a slope on which slump is occurring, step-like depressions are created, and a bulge of earth forms at the base of the slope. A curved scar is left in the area where the material existed before the slump.

Slumps often occur on sea cliffs, the bases of which have been cut away by currents or waves. They can also be seen on slopes that have been eroded by a stream or glacier, as well as those that have been steepened by construction—such as along roads and highways. They are usually triggered by heavy, prolonged rains or earthquakes.

Landslides prompted by heavy rains

One cause of landslides is the saturation of soil on steep slopes, caused by prolonged or heavy rainfall (such as from severe storms) or the melting of large quantities of snow or ice. Once the soil on the surface becomes saturated, the water makes its way down to lower layers. Those layers become slippery at the same time that the surface material is made heavier by the water. At some point, the soil—pulled downward by gravity and lubricated by the water underneath—slides away from the slope. On January 11–13, 1966, for instance, heavy rains gave way to landslides on the mountainsides above Rio de Janeiro, Brazil. The cascading mud and debris killed some 550 people and brought transportation and communication systems to a halt.

Similarly on April 26, 1974, driving rains caused a landslide on a mountain above the Mantaro River in Huancavelica Province, Peru. The falling debris landed on twelve small villages, causing the deaths of 200 to 300 people. It also blocked the river, backing up the water into a natural reservoir 8 miles (13 kilometers) long, 200 yards (183 meters) wide,

Sinkholes

The movement of Earth's surface sometimes takes the form of a vertical drop, in which case a sinkhole is formed. A sinkhole is a large depression in the ground, often shaped like a bowl or a funnel. Sinkholes vary greatly in diameter from several feet to several miles, and may attain depths of 100 feet (30 meters) or more. Some sinkholes become clogged with clay and then collect water, forming small lakes.

One cause of sinkholes is that the underlying layer of water-soluble rock—such as limestone, marble, or dolomite—is dissolved by groundwater. As the rock dissolves, underground spaces form and the support for the ground is reduced. When the spaces grow large or numerous and the remaining rock can no longer hold the land above it, the surface collapses.

Large sinkholes form when cave ceilings weaken, become unable to support the weight of the ground above them, and collapse. Another cause of sinkholes is the depletion of aquifers, which are underground layers of spongy rock, gravel, or sand in which water collects. Aquifers become depleted when the underground water is pumped out of the ground faster than it can be replenished by rainwater. A sinkhole may also be formed when pockets of underground gas escape, such as during an earthquake.

In the United States, sinkholes have caused the greatest damage in Florida, Texas, Alabama, Missouri, Kentucky, Tennessee, and Pennsylvania. The country's largest sinkhole on record, called the "December Giant," formed in the woods near Montevallo, Alabama, in Shelby County, on December 2, 1972. The sinkhole, discovered by hunters, was 425 feet (130 meters) long, 350 feet (107 meters) wide, and 150 feet (45 meters) deep. Two days prior to the discovery, a resident in the vicinity had reported that his house shook, trees broke, and he heard a roaring noise.

In 1981 a large sinkhole formed in Winter Park, Florida. As the ground gave way, a three-bedroom house and three cars were swallowed up. The formation of sinkholes is a growing problem in urban areas of central Florida, as the population grows and underground aquifers become depleted at an alarming rate.

Heavy rains from an El Niño-driven storm caused this 65-foot sinkhole in Balboa Avenue in San Diego, California. REPRODUCED BY PERMISSION OF AP/WORLD WIDE PHOTOS.

and 10 to 20 yards (9 to 18 meters) deep. The landslide caused about $5 million in damages. The greatest cost was for the repair of the Huan-cayo-Ayacucho Highway. In 1990 a rain-induced landslide again occurred in Peru—this time in the village of San Miguel de Río Mayo some 500 miles north of the capital city of Lima. About 200 people were unaccounted for and presumed dead after mud flooded the town.

In the low, rolling mountains capped with red sandstone above the Gros Ventre River in northwestern Wyoming (just south of Grand Teton National Park), several days of heavy rain, coupled with melting snow, caused the largest landslide in U.S. history on June 23, 1925. Some 50 million cubic yards (38 million cubic meters) of rock and debris fell into the Gros Ventre River, creating a 350-foot-high (107-meter-high) natural dam. The 5-mile-long (8-kilometer-long) and 225-foot-deep (68-meter-deep) body of water created behind the dam was named Slide Lake by local residents. On May 18, 1927, almost two years after the landslide, melting snow flooded the river and the dam broke loose. Luckily there had been plenty of advance warning, and most of those living in the area evacuated before floodwaters destroyed their downriver settlement.

Intense rainfall from hurricanes can cause multiple landslides. In August 1969, for instance, Hurricane Camille dumped 27 inches (68 centimeters) of rain on the Appalachian Mountains in central Virginia over an eight-hour period. The soil at the top of steep slopes became saturated and set in motion dozens of debris avalanches. About 150 people were killed by the flowing material. Throughout the region houses were destroyed and roads and bridges were buried or washed out.

Earthquake-generated landslides

Earthquakes that occur in areas with steep slopes can cause the slipping of surface soil and rock and the collapse of cliffs. The shock waves produced by earthquakes send material hurtling downward in violent landslides (also see the chapter on Earthquakes). Earthquake-induced landslides happen in mountainous regions such as China, parts of southern California, Alaska, Turkey, and Iran.

One landslide produced by a severe earthquake occurred in Montana, west of Yellowstone Park, on August 17, 1959. In that case, some 40 million cubic yards (30 million cubic meters) of rock tore off the wall of the Madison River Canyon and slid into the river below at a speed of about 100 miles (160 kilometers) per hour. The rocks killed twenty-six people and blocked the river. A lake 6 miles (9.7 kilometers) long and 180 feet (55 meters) deep was formed in the process. After the landslide, a spillway (passageway near the top of a dam through which water from the reservoir travels when the water level becomes high) was carved out of the natural dam and lined with large blocks of rock, creating sufficient drainage to handle heavy rains and keep the dam from collapsing.

In Kashmir (a state in Southwest Asia adjacent to India and Pakistan) in 1840, an earthquake sparked a landslide that dammed the Indus River, forming a lake about 40 miles (64 kilometers) long and 1,000 feet (300 meters) deep. And in 1949 in Tadzhikistan (then part of the Soviet Union), earthquakes in the Pamir Mountains set off landslides that buried the town of Khait, killing all of its 12,000 residents. Today, Russian seismologists (scientists who study earthquakes) operate a laboratory for earthquake prediction research near Khait.

Landslides triggered by volcanic eruptions

Volcanic eruptions often produce a type of mudflow called a lahar (pronounced LAH-hahr). The material in a lahar is created when volcanic ash mixes with water; the water comes from the melting of snow and glaciers around the volcanic crater (also see the chapter on Volca-

Damage from a 1999 landslide in a residential area in the Philippines.
REPRODUCED BY PERMISSION OF AFP/CORBIS-BETTMAN.

noes). The lahar may be very hot and can travel down the steep sides of a volcano at speeds of 100 miles (160 kilometers) per hour. It can flow for great distances, sweeping up houses and cars, uprooting trees, and burying entire communities.

In May 1980, with the eruption of Mount St. Helens in southern Washington state, came one of the largest landslides in U.S. history. Part of the north face of the mountain blew out and the volcanic ash combined with water from lakes and rivers to form colossal mudflows. The mud blocked rivers and ruined bridges and roads. (Fortunately, the area had been evacuated in advance.) Mud even stopped up the Columbia River—a main thoroughfare to the Pacific Ocean—trapping thirty ocean-going ships downstream.

Lahars resulting from the 1985 eruption of the Nevado del Ruiz volcano in the Colombian Andes struck an area that had not been evacuated, despite warnings from geologists (scientists who study the origin, history, and structure of the Earth). The largest of the mudflows overtook the city

House damaged by a volcanic mudslide in Japan. REPRODUCED BY PERMISSION OF ROGER RESSMEYER/CORBIS-BETTMANN.

World's Deadliest Landslide: Gansu, China

On December 16, 1920, the deadliest landslide in recorded history struck Gansu (formerly Kansu), China, resulting in 180,000 deaths. The cause of the landslide was an earthquake centered near the border with Tibet. The hills and cliffs in the region were treeless and covered with a layer of loess (pronounced LOW-ess or LUSS)—a soft, loosely packed material formed from the yellowish dust of the Gobi Desert. The combination of the bare slopes and the fine dust made the soil highly susceptible to slides.

The shock of the earthquake caused the sides of 100-foot-high (30-meter-high) cliffs to collapse. Falling material barricaded the entrances of mountainside caves, in which many peasants made their homes. The landslide laid waste to ten cities and numerous villages in the valleys.

In one village, the only survivors were a farmer and his two sons. Their plot of land had broken loose from a mountaintop and slid down the slope intact, atop a stream of flowing debris. The day of the Gansu landslides is known in China as *Shan Tso liao*, or "When the mountains walked."

of Armero, where it claimed at least 23,000 lives and left another 20,000 people homeless. In some places the mud was 12 feet (3.7 meters) deep. About 15 square miles (39 square kilometers) of land, including rich farmlands where coffee and rice were grown, were covered by the lahar.

Where landslides occur

Landslides occur throughout the world. They are serious problems in several nations, however, particularly Italy and Japan. More than one thousand urban areas in Italy are in landslide danger-zones. In Japan, thousands of homes are lost and more than 100 people are killed by landslides each year.

In the United States, landslides take place in all fifty states. Across the country, they kill between twenty-five and fifty people and cause $1 billion to $2 billion in damage each year. Landslides are the most prevalent in the Appalachians and Rocky Mountains, as well as along the Pacific Coast. It is estimated that more than 2 million landslides have occurred in the Appalachians, and evidence of past landslides exists on more than 30 percent of the area of West Virginia. In Colorado that figure is eight percent. More than 600 landslides have been distin-

Landslides in Southern California

The mountains of Southern California are prone to mudflows, placing communities on the slopes above and in the valleys below in the danger zone. The slopes are steep and unstable. Much of the soil is barren, since frequent wildfires remove vegetation. Some landslides are triggered by intense storms, which saturate the soil and start it moving downhill. Frequent earthquakes also set landslides in motion.

The deadliest landslide in the region's history occurred in February 1969. During the winter of 1968 to 1969, some 44 inches (112 centimeters) of rain fell on the Los Angeles area over a forty-two-day period. As the record-setting rain (which came after forest fires had cleared the slopes of vegetation the previous summer) fell on the San Gabriel Mountains, it soaked layers of soil and gravel. That material eventually began traveling down the mountainsides, gathering debris as it went. The muddy torrent drowned or buried 100 people and caused about $1 billion in damage. One of the hardest-hit places was the fashionable suburb of Glendora, where the mudslide damaged 160 homes and destroyed 5 others. Mud piled up on the major highway leading into Los Angeles and destroyed citrus groves as far north as Ventura, Santa Barbara, and San Luis Obispo counties.

Another part of the Los Angeles area that has suffered from slides is Portuguese Bend on the Palos Verdes Peninsula. Portuguese Bend is an expensive clifftop housing development overlooking the Pacific Ocean. It was built despite warnings from geologists about the region's instability. The material on the top of the cliffs, on which the houses sit, is sandstone mixed

guished in Utah. And coastal slides are a constant menace in California; the San Gabriel Mountains frequently unleash debris flows that ruin homes in the northern Los Angeles area (see the box on Landslides in Southern California above).

Consequences of landslides

Each year landslides take hundreds of lives and cause billions of dollars of damage throughout the world. Landslides engulf villages and kill people and animals. Falling and sliding rock, soil, and debris flatten houses and cars and uproot trees. Material that spills onto a with a clay material made of hardened volcanic ash—materials that readily absorb water. The layer of rock below is shale, which becomes slippery when wet. The bases of the cliffs are subject to erosion by waves.

In 1956, heavy rains caused the first movement of the cliff tops since the homes went up. From the 1960s through the 1980s the gradual slide was made worse by a series of earthquakes, plus the increased weight from additional homes. In 1969 houses on nearby Point Fermin went sliding into the ocean. By the end of the 1980s, the slide of the cliff top in Portuguese Bend had damaged or destroyed 150 homes—for a total cost of $10 million. Thereafter, new development in Portuguese Bend was halted and a drainage system was put in place to keep the slide from worsening and to protect the remaining houses.

Garage damaged by a 1982 mudslide in California. REPRODUCED BY PERMISSION OF JIM SUGAR PHOTOGRAPHY/CORBIS-BETTMANN.

roadway or railroad tracks halts traffic and causes accidents and sometimes fatalities. And when rocks fall into a lake from high above, they create waves that threaten coastal settlements (see the chapter on Tsunamis).

When a large quantity of material falls, it forces a wall of air ahead of it. That wind may be strong enough to knock down trees and houses. When the material strikes the ground it sends up a cloud of dust that may darken the sky and spread over a large area. Landslides also knock down utility poles and wires, and the region loses power and communication with the outside world. Landslides also scar the face of a hill or mountain—stripping it of soil, trees, and other vegetation.

Rock or soil that flows into a valley often blocks the flow of rivers, thus disrupting ecosystems and shipping routes and sometimes contaminating drinking water. The natural dam may later give way, causing floods.

The human factor

Most of the destructive impacts of landslides are due, in some part, to human activity. Many landslides occur on slopes that have been altered by grading (leveling-off of an area) for road or building construction. When a portion of a mountainside is graded, material is cut out of the slope and removed. The slope directly above the graded area is greatly steepened, reducing support for earth and rock higher up the slope. And if the excavated material is deposited beneath the graded area, it may overload the lower portion of the slope and cause a landslide.

Construction is especially dangerous on slopes that, due to their geologic composition, are unstable (prone to landslides) in their natural state. For example, mountains or cliffs that have a layer of sandstone on the surface and a layer of shale beneath are geologically unstable. Water can seep into pores and cracks in the sandstone and collect on the shale. The shale surface then becomes slippery, allowing the sandstone layer to slide off.

Mining is another activity that weakens slopes and promotes landslides. The removal of coal, stone, or other natural resources from the ground makes the remaining slope unstable and vulnerable to collapse.

Another contribution people make to landslides is cutting down trees on slopes for use as fuel and lumber or to clear the land for farming. Trees protect slopes by trapping rain on their leaves and reducing the erosive impact of wind and water on the soil. The roots of trees and other forms of vegetation absorb rainwater like a sponge and release it slowly into the soil. Roots also act as anchors, holding the soil together. Soil with no vegetative cover erodes quickly. It glides more easily over the rocky subsurface than does compact, cohesive soil. And landslides on deforested slopes, once set in motion, have no natural barriers to slow or stop them. Foot traffic on mountains, from sightseers or recreationists, also tramples vegetation and increases the slopes' vulnerability to landslides.

Technology connection

Technology is of limited usefulness in predicting and preventing landslides. Most large slides occur without warning and are more powerful

The Yosemite Rockfall

On July 10, 1996, a tremendous rockfall shook the ground in Yosemite (pronounced YO-sem-it-ee) National Park in California. Two slabs of an enormous boulder, balanced 2,600 feet (79 meters) above Yosemite Valley on a granite arch, suddenly broke loose. The rocks, weighing 68,000 tons (61,676 metric tons), slid down a steep slope for the first 500 feet (152 meters) and then took to the air and fell freely for the next 1,700 feet (518 meters) until smashing into a rocky slope near the base of the cliff. When the fragmented rocks struck the ground, they were traveling faster than 160 miles (257 kilometers) per hour.

On impact, the rockfall released a wind blast that knocked over hundreds of pine and oak trees and destroyed a nature center and snack bar nearby. The falling trees killed one park visitor and injured several others. The dust from the rockfall and blast of wind blotted out the sky and hung in the air for several hours before settling over an area of about 50 acres (20 hectares).

Rockslide in Yosemite National Park, California.
REPRODUCED BY PERMISSION OF JONATHAN BLAIR/CORBIS-BETTMANN.

than any barrier that can be erected. A California engineer, at a conference in 1980, likened landslide prevention to "trying to hold back the storm tides of the ocean." Nonetheless, numerous measures are used to lessen the impact of landslides, as well as to predict certain kinds of landslides.

Limiting landscape damage

Many methods are used to protect populated areas from material that may fall or slide down a slope. For instance, water drainage systems are employed to keep water from saturating ground that is vulnerable to landslides. Wells are pumped in the potential slide area to keep the rain from overflowing aquifers and soaking the ground. (An aquifer is an underground layer of spongy rock, gravel, or sand in which water collects; for more information see the Drought chapter.)

Trees, shrubs, or grasses are planted on bare slopes to hold the soil in place and to stop material that begins to slide. Terraces (broad, step-like cuts) are constructed on steep slopes, so that falling material or water is only able to travel short distances before landing on a plateau and losing its energy. Loose material is removed from high elevations before it begins rolling down a slope. The bases of slopes on which bulges of material, called a "toes," have formed due to slump are immobilized with walls of rock, concrete, or soil. Strong, wire-mesh fences are secured to some cliff faces above roadways to prevent rocks from falling. Railroads can be protected by electric fences that detect rock falls and communicate the need to halt trains in that section of track.

Another measure undertaken to prevent landslides is the filling-in of cracks that develop in the faces of mountains or hills. And an option for protecting structures in landslide-prone areas is to build retaining walls or earth buttresses along slope bottoms. In some valleys, basins are constructed to trap landslide material. In southern California, for

Rockslide fence near Bolungarvik, Iceland. REPRODUCED BY PERMISSION OF PATRICK BENNETT/CORBIS-BETTMANN.

Housing Development Collapses in the Philippines

On August 3, 1999, following four days of heavy rains that caused widespread flooding throughout eastern Asia, a hillside collapsed in Antipolo City, a suburb of Manila. Thirty-one people were killed as the wall of earth crashed into a housing development; as many as forty others were missing and presumed dead. Twenty-five houses were buried by the landslide, and 378 others were damaged. During that same week in the central Philippines, sixty-one other people died in the flooding.

Filipino officials placed the blame for the landslide on a nearby rock and gravel quarry. They claimed that too much rock had been excavated from the slope too close to the houses, thereby allowing groundwater to reach the ground and soften it. The heavy rains proved to be the final factor that caused the earth to give way and collapse on the houses. Officials also noted that they had issued evacuation warnings when cracks appeared in houses and streets earlier that day, but most residents had ignored the warnings.

Rescuers move debris from collapsed houses in an attempt to rescue victims of a series of landslides in the Philippines in 1999.

instance, a series of 120 football-stadium-sized basins have been excavated along the base of the San Gabriel Mountains to catch rocks and debris. They must be emptied frequently in order to continue catching the falling material.

In Japan, which is home to 10 percent of the world's active volcanoes, walls of steel and concrete—as well as drainage systems—have been constructed on mountainsides to protect valley-dwellers from lahars. Television cameras are employed on some slopes to detect the start of landslides and provide advance warning to people in the path of danger.

Predicting landslides

While most landslides occur without warning, certain types can be predicted. The U.S. Geological Survey, together with the National Weather Service, provides advance warning for landslides that are caused by heavy rains. Both organizations monitor rainfall data and forecasts in areas prone to landslides and issue warnings when the ground is becoming saturated. Landslides that come in the wake of volcanic eruptions can also be predicted. Volcano early warning systems detect rumblings that precede eruptions and, quite likely, volcanic mudflows. People living in the vicinity of a volcano are given plenty of advance warning of the need to evacuate (also see the chapter on Volcanoes).

Assessing the danger of building

When construction is proposed in hilly areas, an assessment is made of the hazards posed by landslides. To determine the stability of the slope and the suitability of the region for construction, researchers conduct geologic explorations (to determine soil and rock properties) and look at the history of landslides in the area. From that information they can predict the frequency with which landslides will occur in the area, as well as the destructive potential of those landslides. Areas where landslides are likely to occur would then be placed off-limits to construction and possibly designated for parkland or other limited use.

For more information

Books

Cornell, James. *The Great International Disaster Book*. New York: Charles Scribner's Sons, 1976, pp. 152–157.

Dasch, E. Julius, ed. *Encyclopedia of Earth Sciences*. New York: Macmillan Library Reference, 1996, pp. 291, 544–547.

Ellen, Stephen. "Landslide and Avalanche." *Academic American Encyclopedia,* Volume 12. Danbury, CT: Grolier Inc., 1998, pp. 192–193.

Feather, Ralph M. Jr., and Susan Snyder. *Earth Science*. New York: Glencoe, 1997, pp. 174–179.

Matthews, William H. III. "Landslide." *Encyclopedia Americana,* Volume 16. Danbury, CT: Grolier Inc., 1998, pp. 720–721.

McPhee, John. "Los Angeles Against the Mountains." *The Control of Nature.* New York: Farrar Straus Giroux, 1989.

Muller, Otto H. "Mass Wasting," in *Gale Encyclopedia of Science,* Volume 4. Farmington Hills, MI: Gale Research, 1996, pp. 2233–2237.

Murck, Barbara W. *Dangerous Earth: An Introduction to Geologic Hazards.* New York: John Wiley & Sons, Inc., 1996.

The National Geographic Desk Reference. Washington, DC: National Geographic Society, 1999, pp. 165–166.

Restless Earth: Disasters of Nature. Washington, DC: National Geographic Society, 1997.

Robinson, Andrew. *Earth Shock: Hurricanes, Volcanoes, Earthquakes, Tornadoes and Other Forces of Nature.* New York: Thames and Hudson, 1993.

Sweeney, Karen O'Connor. *Nature Runs Wild.* Danbury, CT: Franklin Watts Inc., 1979, pp. 42–51.

Walker, Jane. *Avalanches and Landslides.* New York: Gloucester Press, 1992.

Ward, Kaari, ed. *Great Disasters.* Pleasantville, NY: Reader's Digest Association, 1989, pp. 166–167.

Periodicals

Simpson, Sarah. "Raging Rivers of Rock." *Scientific American.* (July 2000): pp. 24–25.

Web sites

"Asian Rains Trigger Deadly Mudslides, Wash Away Crops." *CNN Online.* [Online] http://www.cnn.com/WEATHER/9908/03/asia.floods.05/ (accessed on February 15, 2001).

"Deadly Rivers of Mud Flow Through Southern Italy." *CNN Online.* [Online] http://www.cnn.com/WORLD/europe/9805/06/italy.floods/ (accessed on February 15, 2001).

"Death Toll Rises in Italy's Mudslide Disaster." *CNN Online.* [Online] http://www.cnn.com/WORLD/europe/9805/07/italy.mud/ (accessed on February 15, 2001).

"Dozens Feared Buried in Italian Tide of Mud." *CNN Online.* [Online] http://www.cnn.com/WORLD/europe/9805/06/italy.mud.update/ (accessed on February 15, 2001).

"Frank Slide, Alberta: The Day the Mountain Fell." [Online] http://www3.sympatico.ca/goweezer/canada/frank.htm (accessed on February 15, 2001).

"Hundreds Dead as Flooding Continues Across Asia." *CNN Online.* [Online] http://www.cnn.com/WEATHER/9908/05/asia.floods.02/ (accessed on February 15, 2001).

"Italian Mudslide Survivor Found Buried Up to His Neck." *CNN Online.* [Online] http://www.cnn.com/WORLD/europe/9805/08/italy.mudslides.update/ (accessed on February 15, 2001).

Landslide

"Italy Declares State of Emergency; Mudslide Toll Rises." *CNN Online*. [Online] http://www.cnn.com/WORLD/europe/9805/08/italy.mudslides/index.html (accessed on February 15, 2001).

"Landslides and Snow Avalanches in Canada." *Natural Resources Canada*. [Online] http://sts.gsc.nrcan.gc.ca/page1/geoh/slide.htm (accessed on February 15, 2001).

for more information

Books

Ahrens, C. Donald. *Meteorology Today: An Introduction to Weather, Climate, and the Environment.* 5th ed. St. Paul, MN: West Publishing Company, 1994.

Allaby, Michael. *Droughts.* New York: Facts on File, Inc., 1998.

————. *How the Weather Works: 100 Ways Parents and Kids Can Share the Secrets of the Atmosphere.* Pleasantville, NY: The Reader's Digest Association, Inc., 1995.

Allen, Leslie, et. al. *Raging Forces: Earth in Upheaval.* Washington, DC: National Geographic Society, 1995.

Alth, Max, and Charlotte Alth. *Disastrous Hurricanes and Tornadoes.* New York: Franklin Watts, 1981.

Andryszewski, Tricia. *The Dust Bowl: Disaster on the Plains.* Brookfield, CT: The Millbrook Press, 1984.

Anthes, Richard A. *Meteorology,* 6th ed. New York: Macmillan Publishing Company, 1992.

Armbruster, Ann. *Floods.* New York: Franklin Watts, 1996.

————. *Wildfires.* New York: Franklin Watts, 1996.

Armstrong, Betsey R., and Knox Williams. *The Avalanche Book.* Golden, CO: Fulcrum Publishing, 1992.

Bagnall, Norma Hayes. *On Shaky Ground: The New Madrid Earthquake of 1811–1812.* Columbia, MO: University of Missouri Press, 1996.

Berger, Melvin. *Tornadoes Can Make It Rain Crabs: Weird Facts About Natural Disasters.* New York: Scholastic, 1997.

Bolt, Bruce A. *Earthquakes,* 4th ed. New York: W. H. Freeman, 1999.

Bronson, William. *The Earth Shook, the Sky Burned.* San Francisco, CA: Chronicle Books, 1959; reprinted 1997.

Brown, Walter R., and Norman D. Anderson. *Historical Catastrophes: Snowstorms & Avalanches.* Reading, MA: Addison-Wesley, 1976.

Bruce, Victoria. *No Apparent Danger: The True Story of Volcanic Disaster at Galeras and Nevado Del Ruiz.* New York: HarperCollins, 2001.

For More Information

Burby, Liza N. *Heat Waves and Droughts*. New York: Rosen Publishing Group, 1999.

Cable, Mary. *The Blizzard of '88*. New York: Antheneum, 1988.

Caplovich, Judd. *Blizzard! The Great Storm of '88*. Vernon, CT: VeRo Publishing Company, 1988.

Christian, Spencer. *Spencer Christian's Weather Book*. New York: Prentice-Hall, 1993.

———, and Antonia Felix. *Shake, Rattle, and Roll: The World's Most Amazing Earthquakes, Volcanoes, and Other Forces*. New York: John Wiley & Sons, Inc., 1997.

Cone, Patrick. *Wildfire*. Minneapolis, MN: Carolrhoda Books, Inc., 1997.

Cornell, James. *The Great International Disaster Book*. New York: Macmillan Library Reference, 1980.

Couper, Heather. *Comets and Meteors*. New York: Franklin Watts, 1985.

Cunningham, William P., et al. *Environmental Encyclopedia*. Detroit: Gale Research, 1994.

Dasch, E. Julius, ed. *Encyclopedia of Earth Sciences*. New York: Macmillan Library Reference, 1996.

De Blij, Harm J., et al. *Nature on the Rampage*. Washington, DC: Smithsonian Institution, 1994.

———. *Restless Earth*. Washington, DC: National Geographic Society, 1997.

Decker, Robert, and Barbara Decker. *Volcanoes,* 3rd ed. New York: W. H. Freeman, 1997.

Drohan, Michele Ingber. *Avalanches*. New York: Rosen Publishing Group, 1998.

Dudley, Walter C., and Min Lee. *Tsunami!* Honolulu, HI: University of Hawaii Press, 1998.

Engelbert, Phillis. *Astronomy and Space: From the Big Bang to the Big Crunch*. Farmington Hills, MI: U•X•L, 1997.

———. *The Complete Weather Resource*. Farmington Hills, MI: U•X•L, 1997.

———. *U•X•L Science Fact Finder*. Farmington Hills, MI: U•X•L, 1998.

Erlbach, Arlene. *Blizzards*. Chicago: Children's Press, 1995.

Facklam, Howard, and Margery Facklam. *Avalanche!* New York: Crestwood House, 1991.

Feather, Ralph M. Jr., and Susan Snyder. *Earth Science*. New York: Glencoe, 1997.

Fisher, David E. *The Scariest Place on Earth: Eye to Eye with Hurricanes*. New York: Random House, 1994.

Fishman, Jack, and Robert Kalish. *The Weather Revolution: Innovations and Imminent Breakthroughs in Accurate Forecasting*. New York: Plenum Press, 1994.

Forces of Nature. Alexandria, VA: Time-Life Books, 1990.

Gallant, Roy A. *The Day the Sky Split Apart: Investigating a Cosmic Mystery*. New York: Antheneum Books for Young Readers, 1995.

Gemmell, Kathy. *Storms and Hurricanes*. London, England: Usborne Publishing Ltd., 1995.

Gorrell, Gena K. *Catching a Fire: The Story of Firefighting*. Toronto, ON: Tundra Books, 1999.

Hawkes, Nigel. *New Technology: Structures and Buildings.* New York: Twenty-First Century Books, 1994.

Holford, Ingrid. *Weather Facts & Feats,* 2nd ed. Middlesex, England: Guinness Superlatives Limited, 1982.

Hopping, Lorraine Jean. *Blizzards!* New York: Scholastic Inc., 1998.

Hurt, R. Douglas. *The Dust Bowl: An Agricultural and Social History.* Chicago: Nelson-Hall, 1981.

Kahl, Jonathan D. W. *Weather Watch: Forecasting the Weather.* Minneapolis, MN: Lerner Publications Company, 1996.

Keller, Edward A., and Nicholas Pinter. *Active Tectonics: Earthquakes, Uplift, and Landscape.* Upper Saddle River, NJ: Prentice-Hall, 1996.

Keller, Ellen. *Floods!* New York: Simon Spotlight, 1999.

Knapp, Brian. *Drought.* Austin, TX: Steck-Vaughn, 1990.

———. *Flood.* Austin, TX: Steck-Vaughn, 1990.

Kovach, Robert L. *Earth's Fury: An Introduction to Natural Hazards and Disasters.* New York: Prentice-Hall, 1995.

Kramer, Stephen. *Avalanche.* Minneapolis, MN: Carolrhoda Books, 1992.

Lane, Frank W. *The Violent Earth.* Topsfield, MA: Salem House, 1986.

Larsen, Erik. *Isaac's Storm.* New York: Crown Publishers, 1999.

Lauber, Patricia. *Hurricanes: Earth's Mightiest Storms.* New York: Scholastic Press, 1996.

Lee, Sally. *Hurricanes.* New York: Franklin Watts, 1993.

Longshore, David. *Encyclopedia of Hurricanes, Typhoons and Cyclones.* New York: Facts on File, 2000.

Lutgens, Frederick K., and Edward J. Tarbuck. *The Atmosphere: An Introduction to Meteorology,* 5th ed. Englewood Cliffs, NJ: Prentice-Hall, 1992.

Lydolph, Paul E. *The Climate of the Earth.* Lanham, MD: Rowman & Littlefield Publishers, Inc., 1985.

Lyons, Walter A. *The Handy Weather Answer Book.* Detroit: Visible Ink Press, 1997.

McGraw Hill Encyclopedia of Science and Technology. New York: McGraw-Hill, 1997.

McPhee, John. "Los Angeles Against the Mountains" in *The Control of Nature.* New York: Farrar Straus Giroux, 1989.

McSween, Harry Y., Jr. *Meteorites and Their Parent Planets.* New York: Cambridge University Press, 1999.

Mergen, Bernard. *Snow in America.* Washington, DC: Smithsonian Institution Press, 1997.

Merrick, Patrick. *Avalanches.* Plymouth, MN: Child's World, 1998.

Moran, Joseph M., and Lewis W. Morgan. *Essentials of Weather.* Englewood Cliffs, NJ: Prentice-Hall, 1995.

Murck, Barbara W. *Dangerous Earth: An Introduction to Geologic Hazards.* New York: John Wiley & Sons, Inc., 1996.

The National Geographic Desk Reference. Washington, DC: National Geographic Society, 1999.

Newton, David E. *Earthquakes.* New York: Franklin Watts, 1993.

For More Information

Norton, O. Richard. *Rocks from Space*. Missoula, MT: Mountain Press Publishing Company, 1998.

Otfinoski, Steven. *Blizzards*. New York: Twenty-First Century Books, 1994.

Powers of Nature. Washington, DC: National Geographic Society, 1978.

Poynter, Margaret. *Earthquakes: Looking for Answers*. Hillside, NJ: Enslow Publishers, Inc., 1990.

Ritchie, David. *The Encyclopedia of Earthquakes and Volcanoes*. New York: Facts on File, 1994.

Robinson, Andrew. *Earth Shock: Hurricanes, Volcanoes, Earthquakes, Tornadoes and Other Forces of Nature*. New York: Thames and Hudson, 1993.

Rosenfeld, Jeffrey. *Eye of the Storm: Inside the World's Deadliest Hurricanes, Tornadoes, and Blizzards*. New York: Perseus Publishing, 1999.

Rozens, Aleksandrs. *Floods*. New York: Twenty-First Century Books, 1994.

Sieh, Kerry E., and Simon LeVay. *The Earth in Turmoil: Earthquakes, Volcanoes, and their Impact on Humankind*. New York: W. H. Freeman, 1998.

Simon, Seymour. *Wildfires*. New York: Morrow Junior Books, 1996.

Skinner, Brian J., Barbara W. Murck, and Stephen C. Porter. *Dangerous Earth: An Introduction to Geologic Hazards*. New York: John Wiley & Sons, 1997.

Smith, Howard E. Jr. *Killer Weather: Stories of Great Disasters*. New York: Dodd, Mead & Company, 1982.

Souza, D. M. *Powerful Waves*. Minneapolis, MN: Carolrhoda Books, Inc., 1992.

Stanley, Jerry. *Children of the Dust Bowl: The True Story of the School at Weedpatch Camp*. New York: Crown Publishers Inc., 1992.

Steinbeck, John. *The Grapes of Wrath*. New York: Viking Press, 1939.

Stewart, Gail B. *Drought*. New York: Crestwood House, 1990.

Sussman, Art. *Dr. Art's Guide to Planet Earth: For Earthings Ages 12 to 120*. White River Junction, VT: Chelsea Green Publishing, 2000.

Svobida, Lawrence. *Farming the Dust Bowl: A First-Hand Account from Kansas*. Lawrence, KS: University Press of Kansas, 1986. (Originally published in 1940 by The Caxton Printers, Ltd.)

Tufty, Barbara. *1001 Questions Answered About Hurricanes, Tornadoes, and Other Natural Air Disasters*. New York: Dover Publications, 1987.

Vogt, Gregory L. *Asteroids, Comets, and Meteors*. Brookfield, CT: The Millbrook Press, 1996.

Walker, Jane. *Avalanches and Landslides*. New York: Gloucester Press, 1992.

———. *Famine, Drought and Plagues*. New York: Gloucester Press, 1992.

———. *Tidal Waves and Flooding*. New York: Gloucester Press, 1992.

Ward, Kaari, ed. *Great Disasters*. Pleasantville, NY: Reader's Digest Association, 1989.

Waterlow, Julia. *Flood*. New York: Thomson Learning, 1992.

Watt, Fiona, and Francis Wilson. *Weather and Climate*. London, England: Usborne Publishing Ltd., 1992.

Williams, Jack. *The Weather Book: An Easy-to-Understand Guide to the USA's Weather*. New York: USA Today & Vintage Books, 1992.

Williams, Stanley, and Fen Montaigne. *Surviving Galeras*. New York: Houghton-Mifflin, 2001.

Wood, Leigh. *Fires*. New York: Twenty-First Century Books, 1994.

Wright, Russell G. *Flood!* Menlo Park, CA: Addison-Wesley, 1996.

———. *Tornado!* Menlo Park, CA: Addison-Wesley, 1997.

Zebrowski, Ernest Jr. *Perils of a Restless Planet: Scientific Perspectives on Natural Disasters*. New York: Cambridge University Press, 1997.

Periodicals

Ackerman, Jennifer. "Islands at the Edge." *National Geographic*. (August 1997): pp. 2–31.

Akin, Wallace. "The Great Tri-State Tornado." *American Heritage* (May/June 2000): pp. 32–36.

Allen, Brian. "Capitol Hill Meltdown: While the Nation Sizzles, Congress Fiddles over Measures to Slow Down Future Climate Change." *Time*. (August 9, 1999): p. 56+.

Allen, Keith J. "Dust Storm Causes Eleven Accidents on I-10." *The Arizona Republic*. (July 11, 1997): p. A10.

Alpert, Mark. "Killing Asteroids: Once-Secret Data Shows That Earth Gets Hit More Often Than We Thought." *Popular Mechanics*. (April 1, 1997): p. 40+.

"Amid Death, New Villages Begin Life in Papua New Guinea." Associated Press. (July 23, 1998).

Annin, Peter. "Power on the Prairie: In Minnesota, They're Harvesting the Wind." *Newsweek*. (October 26, 1998): p. 66.

Appenzeller, Tim. "Humans in the Hot Seat." *U.S. News & World Report*. (November 6, 2000): p. 54.

Asphaug, Erik. "The Small Planets." *Scientific American*. (May 2000): pp. 46–55.

"Avalanche!" *National Geographic World* (January 1997). pp. 2–6.

Beardsley, Tim. "Dissecting a Hurricane." *Scientific American*. (March 2000): pp. 80–85.

Begley, Sharon. "He's Not Full of Hot Air." *Newsweek*. (January 22, 1996): pp. 24+.

———. "The Mercury's Rising." *Newsweek*. (December 4, 2000): p. 52.

Bentley, Mace, and Steve Horstmeyer. "Monstrous Mitch." *Weatherwise*. (March/April 1999): pp. 15–18.

Black, Harvey. "Heat: Air Mass Murderer." *Weatherwise*. (Aug./Sept. 1996): pp. 1–12.

———. "Hurricanes: Satellite Enhancements." *Weatherwise*. (Feb./March 1996): pp. 10–11.

"Blizzard Hits Chicago and Drives East." *The New York Times*. (January 27, 1967): p. 22.

Bond, Kathleen. "Church Backs Poor in Drought; Brazil's Leaders Slow to Respond." *National Catholic Reporter*. (August 14, 1998): p. 11+.

For More Information

Borenstein, Seth. "Hottest Years Ever Strengthen the Scientific Case for an Ever-Warming World." Knight-Ridder/Tribune News Service. (January 13, 2000).

Boyle, Sam. "Record-Breaking Blizzard Strands Thousands." Associated Press. (January 27, 1978).

"Bracing for the Big One." *Newsweek* (October 30, 1989): pp. 28–32.

Broad, William J. "Glittering Trillions of Tiny Diamonds Are Shed by the Crash of Asteroids." *The New York Times*. (June 11, 1996): p. B5.

Brown, Kathryn. "Invisible Energy." *Discover.* (October 1999): p. 36.

Brownlee, Shannon, and Laura Tangley. "The Wrath of El Niño." *U.S. News and World Report.* (October 6, 1997).

"California Communities Hardest Hit by Week-Long Storm." U.P.I. (March 3, 1983).

Chacon, Richard. "The Earth Calms, and Recovery Begins." *The Boston Globe* (January 19, 2001): A13.

Chang, Maria L. "Rain Forests: Forests on Fire." *Science World.* (April 13, 1998): p. 6.

Cobb, Jr., Charles E. "Bangladesh, When the Water Comes." *National Geographic.* (June 1993): pp. 118–134.

Cobb, Kathy. "North Dakota, Minnesota: The Forks Continue Flood Recovery Plans." *Fedgazette (Minneapolis).* (July 1998): p. 12+.

Coles, Peter. "All Eyes on El Niño." *UNESCO Courier.* (May 1999): p. 30.

Cutlip, Kimbra. "El Niño 1997–98: Changing the Way We Think About the Weather." *Weatherwise.* (March/April 1998): pp. 12–13.

Davies-Jones, Robert. "Tornadoes." *Scientific American.* (August 1995): pp. 48–53, 56–57.

De Roy, Tui. "Caught in a Melting World." *International Wildlife.* (November/December 2000): pp. 12–19.

"Deforestation Blamed in Part for Mexico Flooding." Associated Press. (September 21, 1998).

Dick, Jason. "Global Warming." *The Amicus Journal.* (Summer 1999): p. 13.

"Disease Threatens Survivors of Wave." *The New York Times.* (July 22, 1998): p. A3.

Doubilet, David. "Galápagos Underwater." *National Geographic.* (April 1999): pp. 32–40.

"Drowning: Bangladesh." *The Economist.* (September 12, 1998): p. 43.

Duffy, James A. "Administration Signs Global Warming Agreement." Knight-Ridder/Tribune News Service. (November 12, 1998).

Dugger, Celia W. "Monsoon Hangs On, Swamping Bangladesh." *The New York Times.* (September 7, 1998): p. A1, A5.

———. "2-Month Flood Breeds Havoc and Diseases in Bangladesh." *The New York Times.* (October 10, 1998): p. A9.

"Earthquake Exacerbates El Salvador's Woes." *The Kansas City Star* (January 19, 2001): B6.

Egan, Timothy. "Why Foresters Prefer to Fight Fire with Fire." *The New York Times.* (August 20, 2000): Sec. 4, p. 5.

Ellis, William S. "Africa's Sahel: The Stricken Land." *National Geographic.* (August 1987): pp. 140–179.

"Enviro-Cars: The Race Is On." *Business Week.* (February 8, 1999): p. 74.

"An Eyewitness Account: 'The Tornado Was Right on Top of Me.'" *Weatherwise.* (August 1985): p. 199.

"Fighting Global Warming with Iron at Sea." *Newsweek.* (October 23, 2000): p. 54.

"Fire Forces 200 from Homes Near Boulder." *The New York Times.* (September 18, 2000): p. A22.

"Fire and Rain." *Time International.* (April 20, 1998): p. 34+.

Fisher, Ian. "Cruelty of the Giant Wave: 'Most of the Children Are Dead.'" *The New York Times.* (July 21, 1998): p. A3.

"Flaming Fury." *Newsweek.* (August 21, 2000): p. 58.

Fox, Stephen. "For a While . . . It Was Fun." *Smithsonian.* (September 1999): pp. 128–130, 132, 134–140, 142.

Galway, Joseph G. "Ten Famous Tornado Outbreaks." *Weatherwise.* (June 1981): pp. 100–109.

Ganguly, Dilip. "Tornado Survivors Lament the Price of Prosperity." Associated Press. (May 17, 1996).

Gehrels, Tom. "Collisions with Comets and Asteroids." *Scientific American.* (March 1996): pp. 54–59.

Gibbs, W. Wayt. "The Search for Greenland's Mysterious Meteor." *Scientific American.* (November 1998). pp. 72–79.

"Global Warming May Be Beneficial." *USA Today Magazine.* (June 2000): p. 10.

González, Frank I. "Tsunami!" *Scientific American.* (May 1999): pp. 56–65.

Gore, Rick. "Andrew Aftermath." *National Geographic.* (April 1993): pp. 2–37.

Graf, Daniel, William Gartner, and Paul Kocin. "Snow." *Weatherwise.* (February/March 1996): pp. 48–52.

Gutierrez, Hector. "I-70 Pileup Lands 10 in Hospitals." *Denver Rocky Mountain News.* (August 15, 1997): p. 50A.

Hall, Roy S. "Inside a Texas Tornado." *Weatherwise.* (January-February 1998): p. 16+.

Hanson-Harding, Alexandra. "Global Warming." *Junior Scholastic.* (November 27, 2000). p. 6.

Hart, Daniela. "Northeast Brazil Faces Famine from Drought." *The Washington Post.* (May 17, 1998): p. A26.

Hayden, Thomas. "Enter La Niña, Smiling." *Newsweek.* (December 14, 1998): p. 59.

Hebert, H. Josef. "Scientists Paint Grim View of Impact on U.S. of Global Warming." Associated Press. (June 9, 2000).

Helvarg, David. "Antarctica: The Ice Is Moving." *E.* (September 2000): p. 33.

———. "Weathering El Niño: Hardest Hit and Perhaps the Most Overlooked, the World's Forests Could Feel the Effects for Generations." *American Forests.* (Autumn 1998): p. 29+.

Henson, Robert. "Hot, Hotter, Hottest: 1998 Raised the Bar for Global Temperature Leaps." *Weath-*

erwise. (March/April 1999): pp. 34–37.

———. "The Intensity Problem: How Strong Will a Hurricane Get?" *Weatherwise.* (September/October 1998): pp. 20–26.

———. "Up to Our Necks: In 1997, the Floods Just Wouldn't Stop." *Weatherwise.* (March/April 1998): pp. 22–25.

Holtz, Robert Lee. "Sliver of Dinosaur-Killing Asteroid Is Believed Found." *Los Angeles Times.* (November 19, 1998): p. A1.

"Hope Dwindles for Missing Victims." *Maclean's.* (January 29, 2001): 28.

Hughes, Patrick, and Douglas Le Comte. "Tragedy in Chicago." *Weatherwise.* (Feb./March 1996): pp. 18–20.

"Hurricane Havoc in Central America." *The Economist.* (November 7, 1998): p. 33.

"Hurricanes Rip Through Impoverished Caribbean, Central American Regions." *National Catholic Reporter.* (November 20, 1998): p. 12.

"India Trembles: After Its Worst Earthquake in a Half-Century, the Subcontinent Struggles to Find the Dead, Care for the Survivors and Rebuild Smacked-Down Cities." *Time* (February 5, 2001): 46+.

Iocavelli, Debi. "Hurricanes: Eye Spy." *Weatherwise.* (Aug./Sept. 1996): pp. 10–11.

"It's 'Blow Season' on the Plains." Knight-Ridder/Tribune News Service. (January 19, 1999).

Jehl, Douglas. "Clinton Calls for More Aid to Cure Wildfire Problems." *The New York Times.* (September 10, 2000): p. 24.

Johnson, Tim. "Battered by El Niño, South American Sea Lions and Seals Succumb to Hunger." *The Miami Herald.* (July 28, 1998).

Kaplan, David A. "This Is Global Warming?" *Newsweek.* (January 22, 1996): pp. 20+.

Lescaze, Lee. "'Classic Nor'easter' Sweeps Up the Coast." *Washington Post.* (February 7, 1978): pp. A1, A6.

Kiester, Jr., Edwin. "Battling the Orange Monster." *Smithsonian.* (July 2000): pp. 32–42.

Koop, David. "Wild Child: Although It's Called a Child, 'El Niño' Threatens to Severely Disrupt Weather Patterns." Associated Press. *(June 1997).*

Langreth, Robert. "Asteroid Watchers." *Popular Science.* (September 1992): pp. 76–80, 82.

Lawless, Jill. "Global Warming Threatens a Third of World's Habitats." Associated Press. (August 30, 2000).

Le Comte, Douglas. "Going to Extremes: 1995 Was Wild and Woolly for the U.S." *Weatherwise.* (Feb./March 1996): p. 14+.

———. "Weather Around the World: A Year of Epic Disasters." *Weatherwise.* (March/April 1998): pp. 29–33.

———. "Weather Highlights: Around the World 1997." *Weatherwise.* (March/April 1998): pp. 26–31.

———. "The Weather of 1997: The Year of the Floods." *Weatherwise.* (March/April 1999): pp. 14–21.

———. "The Weather of 1998: A Warm, Wet, and Stormy Year."

Weatherwise. (March/April 1999): pp 19–21.

Leary, Warren E. "Trailblazing Craft Exposes an Asteroid." *The New York Times*. (February 18, 2000): p. A20.

Levine, Mark. "A Storm at the Bone: A Personal Exploration into Deep Weather." *Outside Magazine*. (November 1998).

Linden, Eugene. "Smoke Signals: Vast Forest Fires Have Scarred the Globe, but the Worst May Be Yet to Come." *Time*. (June 22, 1998): p. 50+.

"A Look at the 1925 'Tri-States Tornado.'" Associated Press. (March 17, 2000).

MacKinnon, Ian. "Nothing Between Earth and Sky." *Newsweek International* (February 5, 2001).

Maran, Stephen P. "Comets, Asteroids and Earth. Movie Myths vs. Scientific Reality." *The Washington Post*. (August 12, 1998): p. H1.

Maugh, Thomas H. II. "Eyeballing an Asteroid." *Los Angeles Times*. (December 24, 1998): p. B2.

Mazza, Patrick. "Global Warming Is Here!" *Earth Island Journal*. (Fall 1999): p. 14.

———. "The Invisible Hand: As Human Activity Warms the Earth, El Niño Grows More Violent." *Sierra*. (May-June 1998): p. 68+.

McCarthy, Daniel, and Joseph T. Schaefer. "Tornadoes of 1998: The Deadliest Year in Over Two Decades." *Weatherwise*. (March/April 1999): pp. 32–47.

McKibbin, Warwick J., and Peter J. Wilcoxen. "Until We Know More About Global Warming, the Best Policy Is a Highly Flexible One." *The Chronicle of Higher Education*. (July 2, 1999): p. B4+.

Mohan, Palani. "Papua New Guinea." *Life*. (September 1998): p. 20.

Monastersky, Richard. "Florida Air Loaded with African Dust." *Science News*. (June 14, 1997): p. 373.

Mulvaney, Kieran. "Alaska: The Big Meltdown." *E*. (September 2000): p. 36.

"Murderous Mitch." *Time*. (November 16, 1998): p. 66.

Mydans, Seth. "Southeast Asia Chokes on Indonesia's Forest Fires." *The New York Times*. (September 25, 1997) pp. A1, A14.

Nash, J. Madeleine. "Floods and Fires? They're Just the Beginning of El Niño's Impact." *Time*. (June 1, 1998): p. 26.

———. "Still Waiting for the Big One." *Time* (October 30, 1989): pp. 44–45.

"New Controls Tamed in Nevada Floods, Experts Say." *The New York Times*. (July 10, 1999): p. A9.

Nieves, Evelyn. "Olympia Bears Quake's Scars, Deep or Subtle." *The New York Times*. (March 2, 2001).

Nuttall, Nick. "Ganges Glacier 'Melting Fast.'" *The Times* (London). (July 20, 1999): p. 9.

Ocko, Stephanie. "Sea Change: The Birth of an El Niño." *Weatherwise*. (December 1997): p. 16.

"Operation Rescue." *Time*. (June 1, 1998): p. 26.

"Papua New Guinea Says Fewer Lost from Waves." *The New York Times*. (July 26, 1998): p. A9.

Parfitt, Michael. "The Essential Element of Fire." *National Geographic.* (September 1996): pp. 116–139.

———. "Living with Natural Hazards." *National Geographic.* (July 1998): pp. 2–39.

Pearce, Fred. "The Real Green Revolution." *New Scientist.* (December 13, 1997): p. 53.

———. "Science: Meltdown in the Mountains." *The Independent* (London). (March 31, 2000): p. 8.

Pennisi, Elizabeth. "Dancing Dust; Scientists Seek the Secrets of Dust Storms." *Science News.* (October 3, 1992): p. 218+.

Perkins, S. "Greenland's Ice Is Thinner at the Margins." *Science News.* (July 22, 2000): p. 54.

Peterson, Chester Jr. "Harvest the Wind: The Midwest Could Be the Saudi Arabia of Wind-Powered Energy." *Successful Farming.* (January 1999): p. 44+.

Petri, Bob. "Get Off Highway Before Dust Hits." *The Arizona Republic.* (July 9, 1999): p. B2.

Proctor, Paul. "Fire-Fighting Fleet Stretched to Limit as U.S. West Burns." *Aviation Week & Space Technology.* (August 21, 2000): pp. 38–39.

Rasicot, Julie. "Locals Help Battle Fires in Montana; Despite Risk, Hardship, 'I'd Go Back in a Minute.'" *The Washington Post.* (August 17, 2000): p. 16.

Rauss, Uli. "After the Fires." *World Press Review.* (March 1998): p. 39.

Reville, William. "The Fireball That May Have Doomed the Dinosaur." *The Irish Times.* (September 21, 1998): p. 7.

———. "Why It May Have Taken More Than an Asteroid 65 Million Years Ago to Wipe Out the Dinosaur." *The Irish Times.* (August 30, 1999): p. 7.

Revkin, Andrew C. "Treaty Talks Fail to Find Consensus in Global Warming." *The New York Times.* (November 26, 2000).

Rosenfeld, Jeff. "The Forgotten Hurricane." *Weatherwise.* (Aug./Sept. 1993): pp. 13–18.

———. "Unearthing Climate." *Weatherwise.* (May 2000): p. 12.

Samad, Ataus. "Bangladesh Struggles to Resurface from Storm." *Christian Science Monitor.* (May 10, 1989): p. 6.

"Scientist Says He Found Piece of Asteroid That Killed Dinosaurs." *The New York Times.* (November 19, 1998): p. A21.

Shabe, John. "The Good, the Bad, the Soggy." *Contact Kids.* (November 1998): p. 8.

Shacham, Mordechai. "Danger by the Numbers: Meaningful Cold Weather Indicators." *Weatherwise.* (Oct./Nov. 1995): pp. 27–28.

Shilts, Elizabeth. "Harnessing a Powerful Breeze." *Canadian Geographic.* (May-June 1999): p. 20.

Simpson, Sarah. "Raging Rivers of Rock." *Scientific American.* (July 2000): pp. 24–25.

"Six Are Killed and 200 Injured as Tornadoes Strike Midwest." *The New York Times.* (January 25, 1967): p. 28.

"6 Die in Pileup as Storm Closes Road." *The Seattle Times.* (September 26, 1999): p. B3.

Stange, Mary. "Tinder Dry: The Old West." *USA Today*. (August 24, 2000): p. A15.

"The State of U.S. Renewable Power." *Mother Earth News*. (February 1999): p. 16.

Stevens, William K. "Catastrophic Melting of Ice Sheet Is Possible, Studies Hint." *The New York Times*. (July 7, 1998): p. B13.

———. "Harmful Heat Is More Frequent, Especially at Night, Study Finds." *The New York Times*. (December 10, 1998): p. A1.

———. "Human Imprint on Climate Change Grows Clearer." *The New York Times*. (June 29, 1999): p. 1+.

———. "Persistent and Severe, Drought Strikes Again." *The New York Times*. (April 25, 2000): pp. D1, D4.

Sudetic, Chuck. "As the World Burns." *Rolling Stone*. (September 2, 1999): p. 97+.

Suplee, Curt. "El Niño/La Niña: Nature's Vicious Cycle." *National Geographic*. (March 1999): pp. 72–95.

"Taken by the Wind." *People Weekly*. (May 31, 1999): p. 105+.

"That Dreadful Smog Is Back." *The Economist*. (March 18, 2000): p. 40.

Thompson, Liz. "California and the West: The Odds of Getting Hit By an Asteroid." *Los Angeles Times*. (July 28, 1999): p. A3.

"Troubled on the Sea Islands." *Scholastic Update*. (September 20, 1996): p. 15+.

"United Front Against Wildfires." *Los Angeles Times*. (September 20, 2000): p. B8.

"U.S. Signs Kyoto Pact." *Maclean's*. (November 23, 1998): p. 93.

Van Biema, David. "The Blizzard of '96." *Time*. (January 22, 1996): pp. 18+.

Vandas, Steve. "Coastal Hazards: Hurricanes, Tsunamis, Coastal Erosion." *Science Scope*. (May 1998): pp. 28–31.

Verhovek, Sam Howe. "Big Quake Jolts Northwest; Damage Estimated in Billions." *The New York Times*. (March 1, 2001).

———. "Sighs of Relief and Gasps at Earthquake's Cost in Western Washington." *The New York Times*. (March 2, 2001).

"When the Smoke Clears in Asia." *The Economist*. (October 4, 1997): p. 43+.

Whitmore, Stuart. "Wave of Woes." *Asiaweek*. (July 31, 1998): p. 28.

"Wildfire Grows Rapidly Near Yellowstone Park." *The New York Times*. (August 15, 2000): p. 21.

Williams, Jack. "Watching the Vapor Channel: Satellites Put Forecasters on the Trail of Weather's Hidden Ingredient." *Weatherwise*. (Aug./Sept. 1993): pp. 26–30.

Williams, A. R. "After the Deluge." *National Geographic*. (November 1999): pp. 108–129.

Zimmer, Carl. "The El Niño Factor." *Discover*. (January 1999): pp. 98–106.

Zumbo, Jim. "The Big Chill." *Outdoor Life*. (September 1997): pp. 12+.

Websites

American Meteorological Society Homepage. [Online] http://www.

ametsoc.org (accessed April 27, 2001).

The Borneo Project. Earth Island Institute. [Online] http://www.earth island.org/borneo/ (accessed March 8, 2001) .

Canadian Avalanche Association. [Online] http://www.avalanche.ca (accessed January 17, 2001).

The Canadian Wildfire Network. [Online] http://www.denendeh.com/fly color/wildfire (accessed December 8, 2000).

Climate Prediction Center. National Centers for Environmental Prediction and the National Weather Service. [Online] http://www.cpc.ncep.noaa. gov/ (accessed April 27, 2001).

Colorado Avalanche Information Center. [Online] http://www.caic. state.co.us/ (accessed January 18, 2001).

Complete Text of Rio Declaration. Agenda for Change. [Online] http:// www.igc.apc.org/habitat/agenda21/ rio-dec. html (accessed February 12, 2001).

Cyberspace Snow and Avalanche Center. [Online] http://www.csac.org (accessed January 18, 2001).

Disaster News Network. [Online] http://www.disasternews.net (accessed April 18, 2001).

Discovery Channel Online. [Online] http://www.discovery.com/area/ history/dustbowl/dustbowl1.1.html (accessed January 23, 2001).

Earthquake Hazards Program. U.S. Geological Society. [Online] Available http://earthquake.usgs.gov/ (accessed April 26, 2001).

Earthquake Information. [Online] http: //www-geology.ucdavis.edu/eq mandr.html (accessed January 19, 2001).

Earthquake Information from the USGS. U.S. Geologic Survey. [Online] http://quake.wr.usgs.gov/ (accessed January 19, 2001).

El Niño and Climate Prediction. National Oceanic and Atmospheric Administration. [Online] http://www. pmel.noaa.gov/toga-tao/el-nino- report.html (accessed March 8, 2001).

El Niño-Southern Oscillation Page." National Oceanic and Atmospheric Administration. [Online] http://www. elnino.noaa.gov/ (accessed March 8, 2001).

Environmental News Network. [Online] http://www.enn.com/special reports/elnino/ (accessed March 8, 2001).

EQE Earthquake and Natural Hazards Site. [Online] http://www.eqe.com/ index.html (accessed January 19, 2001).

Explorezone. [Online] http://explore zone.com (accessed February 27, 2001).

Federal Emergency Management Agency Library. [Online] http://www. fema.gov/library (accessed March 2, 2001).

FEMA for Kids. [Online] http://www. fema.gov/kids (accessed March 8, 2001).

Firehouse.com Wildfire News. [Online] http://www.firehouse.com/wild fires (accessed March 6, 2001).

Flood-Zone.Net. [Online] http://www. flood-zone.net/index.htm (accessed April 26, 2001).

Frank Slide, Alberta: The Day the Mountain Fell. [Online] http://www3.sympatico.ca/goweezer/canada/frank.htm (accessed February 15, 2001).

Gallatin National Forest Avalanche Center. [Online] http://www.mtavalanche.com (accessed January 18, 2001).

Global Earthquake Response Center. [Online] http://www.earthquake.org (accessed April 28, 2001).

Great 1906 San Francisco Earthquake. [Online] http://quake.wr.usgs.gov/more/1906 (accessed January 19, 2001).

Impacts of El Niño and Benefits of El Niño Prediction. National Oceanic and Atmospheric Administration. [Online] http://www.pmel.noaa.gov/toga-tao/el-nino/impacts.html (accessed March 8, 2001).

Index of Tsunamis. University of Washington Geophysics Program. [Online] http://www.geophys.washington.edu/tsunami/general/historic/ (accessed March 4, 2001).

Johnstown Pennsylvania Information Source Online. [Online] http://www.johnstownpa.com (accessed March 8, 2001).

Johnstown Flood Museum. [Online] http://www.jaha.org (accessed March 8, 2001).

Landsat. National Aeronautic and Space Administration. [Online] http://spacelink.nasa.gov/NASA.Projects/Earth.Science/Land/Landsat/ (accessed December 18, 2000).

Museum of the City of San Francisco. [Online] http://www.sfmuseum.org (accessed January 19, 2001).

NASA Tsunami Observatorium. [Online] http://observe.ivv.nasa.gov/nasa/exhibits/ tsunami/ (accessed March 4, 2001).

National Centers for Environmental Prediction. National Oceanic and Atmospheric Administration and the National Service. [Online] http://www.ncep.noaa.gov (accessed April 28, 2001).

National Climatic Data Center. [Online] http://www.ncdc.noaa.gov (accessed March 8, 2001).

National Drought Mitigation Center. [Online] http://enso.unl.edu/ndmc/ (accessed January 22, 2001).

National Geophysical Data Center. [Online] http://www.ngdc.noaa.gov (accessed March 4, 2001).

National Hurricane Center. [Online] http://www.nhc.noaa.gov (accessed March 8, 2001).

National Snow and Ice Data Center. [Online] http://www.nsidc.colorado.edu/NSDIC/EDUCATION/BLIZZARD/intro.html (accessed January 22, 2001).

National Wildfire Coordinating Group. [Online] http://www.nwcg.gov (accessed December 8, 2000).

Natural Disaster Reference Database. [Online] http://ltpwww.gsfc.nasa.gov/ndrd (accessed April 18, 2001).

Natural Resources Conservation Service. [Online] http://www.nc.nrcs.usda.gov (accessed January 23, 2001).

NEAR Science Update. John Hopkins NEAR Website. [Online] http://near.jhuapl.edu/news/sci_updates/00oct03.html (accessed February 27, 2001).

NOAA El Niño Page. National Oceanic and Atmospheric Administration. [Online] http://www.elnino.noaa.gov/ (accessed March 8, 2001).

For More Information

For More Information

NOAA's Drought Information Center. [Online] http://www.drought.noaa.gov/ (accessed January 22, 2001).

Northeast Regional Climate Center. [Online] http://met-www.cit.cornell.edu/nrcc_home.html (accessed January 22, 2001).

Northwest Weather and Avalanche Center. [Online] http://www.nwac.noaa.gov (accessed January 19, 2001).

NOVA Online. [Online] http://www.pbs.org/wgbh/nova (accessed March 8, 2001).

Outlook: Tornadoes. National Oceanic and Atmospheric Administration. [Online] http://www.outlook.noaa.gov/tornadoes (accessed March 2, 2001).

Savage Earth Online. PBS and the Corporation for Public Broadcasting. [Online]. http://www.pbs.org/wnet/savageearth/ (accessed April 18, 2001).

SG's Monsoon Page. [Online] http://theory.tifr.res.in/~sgupta/others/monsoon.html (accessed December 30, 2000).

Spacekids. [Online] http://www.spacekids.com (accessed February 27, 2001).

Spacezone: Astronomy News and Reference. *Explorezone*. [Online] http://explorezone.com/space/ (accessed February 27, 2001).

Storm Chaser Homepage. [Online] http://www.stormtrack.org (accessed March 2, 2001).

Storm Prediction Center. National Oceanic and Atmospheric Administration, National Weather Service, and the National Centers for Environmental Prediction. [Online] http://www.spc.noaa.gov (accessed April 26, 2001).

Stormfax Weather Almanac. [Online] http://www.stormfax.com/ (accessed March 8, 2001).

Students for the Exploration and Development of Space. [Online] http://seds.lpl.arizona.edu (accessed February 27, 2001).

Surfing the Internet for Earthquake Data. [Online] http://www.geophys.washington.edu/seismosurfing.html (accessed January 19, 2001).

Surviving the Dust Bowl. PBS Online: The American Experience. [Online] http://www.pbs.org/wgbh/amex/dustbowl/ (accessed January 23, 2001).

Tidal Wave Destroys Villages, Kills 70 in Papua New Guinea. CNN Interactive. [Online] http://www.cnn.com/WORLD/asiapcf/9807/18/tidal.wave/ (accessed March 4, 2001).

The Tornado Project Online. [Online] http://www.tornadoproject.com (accessed March 2, 2001).

1925 Tri-State Tornado Web Page. National Oceanic and Atmospheric Administration. [Online] http://www.crh.noaa.gov/pah/1925/ (accessed March 2, 2001).

Tsunami Program. National Oceanic and Atmospheric Administration. [Online] http://www.pmel.noaa.gov/tsunami/ (accessed March 4, 2001).

Understanding Earthquakes. [Online] http://www.crustal.ucsb.edu/ics/understanding (accessed January 19, 2001).

USA Today Weather. USA Today. [Online] http://www.usatoday.com/weather/ (accessed March 8, 2001).

The Weather Channel. [Online] http://www.weather.com/weather_center (accessed March 2, 2001).

Westwide Avalanche Network. [Online] http://www.avalanche.org (accessed January 19, 2001.)

Wildfire News. [Online] http://www.wildfirenews.com (accessed December 8, 2000).

Wind Erosion Research Unit. U.S. Department of Agriculture [Online] http://www.weru.ksu.edu/ (accessed January 23, 2001).

Winds of Destruction Homepage. The Weather Channel. [Online] http://www. weather.com/weather_center/special_report/tornado/index.html (accessed March 2, 2001).

Yucatan Impact Crater Site. National Aeronautics and Space Administration. [Online] http://www.jpl.nasa.gov/radar/sircxsar/yucatan.html (accessed February 27, 2001).

For More Information

index